East to West

East to West

The Early Years

ELIZABETH GREEN

ISIS
LARGE PRINT
Oxford

Copyright © E. Green, 2004

First published in Great Britain 2004
by
Bound Biographies Limited

Published in Large Print 2005 by ISIS Publishing Ltd.,
7 Centremead, Osney Mead, Oxford OX2 0ES
by arrangement with the author c/o
Bound Biographies Limited

British Library Cataloguing in Publication Data
Green, Elizabeth
    East to west : the early years. – Large print ed.
    (Isis reminiscence series)
    1. Green, Elizabeth – Childhood and youth
    2. Large type books
    3. Great Britain – Social life and customs
    – 1918–1945
    4. London (England) – Biography
    I. Title
    942.1'083'092

ISBN 0–7531–9330–2 (hb)
ISBN 0–7531–9331–0 (pb)

Printed and bound in Great Britain by
T. J. International Ltd., Padstow, Cornwall

Dedicated with love to my dear husband Bob,
and to the whole family, especially
my precious children Vivien and Lionel.

CONTENTS

Acknowledgements ix

1. A Grand Entrance 1

2. The Shop 10

3. The World Outside 21

4. The Extended Family and Neighbours ... 40

5. Enter Leonard 62

6. A Miscellany of Memories 82

7. Additions and Subtractions 105

8. The Scholarship 125

9. The Grammar School 148

10. Threats and Rumours of War 169

ACKNOWLEDGEMENTS

With grateful thanks to my tireless and helpful husband Bob, and my encouraging copy readers, Mignon and Dorothy, who inspired me to continue, Grandpa and Grandma Pritchard, my maternal grandparents, and Grandfather and Grandmother Cronk.

CHAPTER ONE

A Grand Entrance

I remember, I remember,
The house where I was born,
The little window where the sun
Came peeping in at dawn.

Thomas Hood

Being born, I am assured, isn't that easy, and I truly cannot really remember, but I do know that finding the right parents and most suitable environment is more difficult. The success rate among babies in this field is not very high. To me, an appearance in the East End of London in the 1920s was certainly a debatable choice. Yet I was fortunate to have a mother who wanted me and who made definite if frugal preparations for my arrival. Also I was blessed with a father who, although not a good businessman, did at least love his little daughter and tried to provide for his family and keep the wolf from the door. My father, Percival Cronk, more commonly known as "Perc", was 43 when I put in an appearance, and my mother Gladys, née Pritchard, was 13 years his junior.

Like the Queen, I was born in 1926; my third name was Elizabeth and, like her today, we then lived over the shop. There the similarity ended. Mine was a real shop and not a very prosperous one. Our whole establishment would have comfortably fitted into one of the state rooms, and in splendour and opulence was as different as chalk from cheese. However, until the mass exodus from cities at the beginning of the Second World War, that little back street tobacconist/confectioner's-cum-grocer's emporium set amongst a number of tiny terraced workmen's cottages was my home.

Trade was never very brisk even in the early years. Father had sadly bought a "pig in a poke" and spent all his money in the process. My poor mother soon had to do part-time work, mostly charring or taking in washing, to help swell the family's budget and boost the shop's takings. My impoverished parents always hoped for better days which sadly never came, but for a while, until I was eight, our affairs progressed fairly smoothly and were not too stretched. We all rubbed along reasonably well with enough spare time and a little spare cash for inexpensive treats and outings.

As my mother was often out working, it was my underworked father who mainly cared for me during the daytime. Now I realise he was old enough to be my grandfather and had the patience and attitude of one. With sporadic business activity and little going into the till, he gave much of his leisure, and great paternal love, to his inquisitive growing child.

Eden Road was certainly a misnomer, and bore no resemblance to its Biblical reference. The properties there were closely compacted together, but each residence had its own minute railing-enclosed front garden and, for such an area in a busy metropolis, a quite reasonable narrow patch behind, overlooked by similar houses.

Our business premises had a concrete approach and no railings. Every family in the street had a treasured, infrequently used, front room except us. Two murky bay windows displayed our wares and our front door always had to be open. Shelves and a counter took the place of a settee and armchairs, and cracked dark brown linoleum substituted for their very flowery carpets. How I longed for a closed front door, and even more so for a special front room!

Through the dwellings and beyond the scullery, everyone had a cemented backyard, leading to the outside and only lavatory. Ours was a very untidy area with buckets, mops and balding brooms propped up against the walls. The wringer took pride of place, blocking any view from our living room. It was covered with old rags and mackintoshes. Several tin baths hung on the fence between us and our neighbours.

We had no lush green lawn, but a semblance of a very small field of long uneven grass and weeds. We grew neither vegetables nor cultivated flowers, but regularly each summer a few wild flowers gave the only colour there, plus a spreading loganberry bush. How that plant flourished is difficult to believe, yet its delicious fruit gave many treats during hot days. For a young only child with quite a good imagination and knowledge of no other, this garden was paradise, and I revelled in its undergrowth.

My parents were very different in outlook and background. This fact was evident even to me when I was quite small. Frequent arguments, intensified by lack of money, disturbed our peace. Happiness abounded when they were speaking and pleasant with each other; uncertainty and insecurity prevailed when outbursts were followed by continual sullen silences from my father which often took days to dispel.

The early picture of my mother was of a fairly slim jolly person always dashing about. She seemed very cheerful with a constant smile; her eyes were bright and dark brown, her hair thick and slightly wavy. Printed on my very early memory is the almost black carpet on the kitchen floor made by her lovely tresses after her first short bob, then all the fashion. Great fears filled her daughter when her friend went to singe the new ends. I rushed to pull her away, dreading that at any moment my mother would catch fire. Apparently the current belief was that newly cut strands bled; burning supposedly prevented this happening!

At that time my mother was forever laughing and singing. Her youth had been in the era of the Crystal Palace choirs, and she filled the house with favourite pieces from the competitions she had entered. Sadly, this happy vision of her dimmed as finances grew less stable, and she became bogged down with real poverty and endless work.

Superstitions ruled all our lives. There were reasons for almost everything done or left undone. For Mother,

4

crossed knives were a portent of future quarrels; spilt salt had to be thrown over a particular shoulder; umbrellas must never be opened indoors; no shoes put on tables in case of bad luck and so it went on. I soon learned that if I wanted anything desperately, then Mother must be asked. She wished to please, regardless of the suitability of the request, and she would reply quickly before Father even knew it had been mentioned. Clever with her needle and good at simple sewing tasks, Mum made all my clothes and underclothes, except coats which were second-hand and that article called a liberty bodice. This strange contraption was a type of chest protector, worn on cold days, with rubber buttons on lower edges to which suspenders were attached. These kept up thick, black, very itchy stockings, the scourge of all schoolgirls in wintertime.

During the summer we often had matching dresses made from cheap remnants, which made me feel very grown up and so companionable. Any unworn corners of my mother's petticoats or top garments, and the good parts of my father's shirts, were utilised for my needs and looked quite professional trimmed with unpicked lace. Discarded jumpers from kindly relatives and friends were unravelled many times and then re-knitted to keep up with my growth. One very pretty variegated green adult cardigan was remade five successive times to fit me between five and twenty years. It was a sad loss when carelessly it got left behind on a college expedition.

On the other hand my father was most impractical — he couldn't knock in the proverbial nail. He was the quiet, serious and studious one. His expression was mainly solemn and worried, yet how rewarding was his occasional lovely smile. As I grew older he surprised me several times with his dry, almost unnoticed, sense of humour, but gradually financial failure deprived him of this safety valve.

He was shorter than his wife, very thin, and he always wore glasses. His sight was poor and he suffered from constant headaches — now I realise he could have been a migraine sufferer. Dad very seldom left the shop, which only shut on Thursday and Sunday afternoons, often reopening during the evenings. It was a red-letter day if he ever accompanied my mother and me on an outing; he never ever went out with his wife alone. His only pleasure seemed to be putting the world to rights with his few local elderly cronies who came up to the counter more for a chat than to purchase goodies.

My father's wonderful patience and willingness to explain things was much overused by me but was only truly appreciated when I was almost an adult. Right from its commencement he was interested in my school life and would help me whenever possible. As I went to my mother for light quick decisions, so for really important difficult problems that required studied and thoughtful answers, my approach then was to him. Sadly, because my mother was always so busy and weary when she was at home, and my father was mostly underemployed with so few customers, and with me most of the day, I got to know him when very young better than I did her. Naturally, I looked to him far more for attention and help, and I was generally known as "Daddy's girl".

Until just before the First World War, my father had always lived in a small country town. One of the younger sons of a family of eight boys and an only girl, he had shone in the local school and they had all been regular church members, all the sons singing in the choir. Grandfather had been coachman to the local vicar and my father grew up loving horses. What he had seen and heard wandering in the fields and driving round the gentle Surrey lanes, he elaborated in the many tales he spun for his eager listener.

My father must have hated being cooped up in that crowded backwater in the East End, and disliked intensely working patchily in that dingy shop. Unfortunately his increasingly poor health and pressing worries, due to lack of money, drained his vitality and prevented him visiting old haunts, or even venturing into Epping Forest only ten minutes away from Eden Road. He never complained about the sad changes in his surroundings, but his wistful remembrances showed clearly how he longed for the old country life. Sadly, too, his resentment must have been the cause of much of his sulkiness and arguments with my mother. Yet, although realising his failure to make a reasonable living for his family, he lacked the ideas and practical abilities to do anything to improve matters himself.

There was a pride and independence of spirit and some hope in those early days, but gradually all was worn away. Reading offered an escape and so did my father's daily discussions with his customers about local and national politics. These activities were not shared by his wife — she never realised his love of country things, his delight in books and friendly verbal arguments. Nor did he understand her love of town life, and need for continual change, for highlights and drama, and her constant desire for company. How fortunate I consider myself to have inherited their diverse traits, even though these may have been the source of my parents' incompatibility.

In complete contrast my mother was a true lively cockney, inclined to be feckless, and the instigator of many of her own problems yet very optimistic and extremely generous of thought — also, she never held a grudge. Everything was dramatised, probably to counteract the drabness of our none-too-exciting back street existence. Had there been enough cash, she would have wished to dress well, eat out occasionally, visit friends and relatives more often and have visitors to our home frequently. Also she would have spent some time at shows and theatres. In those days very few ordinary folk could indulge in such activities as we do now; my parents certainly hadn't the time or money to do so. Perhaps my early attempts in Sunday School tableaux and school plays helped to compensate a little. My mother certainly supported me by her wonderful efforts with the costumes and by attending every possible performance. Sadly, had my father had more "go" in him to improve their circumstances, she would have been a wonderful helper, able to give him a lot of practical support.

For nearly eight years I was an only child, lonely, rather withdrawn and quiet; lacking both the happy-go-lucky nature of one parent and the very tense, serious and occasionally sullen attitude of the other. Yet I was blessed during that time with the practical care of my mother and the almost undivided attention of my father and the love of both of them. This then was the backdrop to the first 13 years of my life.

CHAPTER
TWO

The Shop

England is a nation of shopkeepers.
Napoleon

Our shop seemed a big dark secret and a forbidding place and, for a very small child, exploration was impossible — when I could first walk I was far too scared to venture there on my own. During daylight hours, even with adults around, it was an area to scurry furtively through, with held breath, clenched hands and almost closed eyes. Alarming shapes and indeterminate forms seemed to be lurking in all the deep corners that set the heart pounding and dried up the mouth. When the business day was over, the street door firmly shut, the dull light switched off and we were all safe in the back kitchen, I then felt a little happier and could almost forget that ghostly place. Even with the dividing glass partition tightly curtained, just thinking about those spectred haunts and shadowy recesses could result in nightmares. At least there were comforting arms and calm words to console me whenever I called out in fright in those very early days.

Looking back over the years it always seemed wintertime in that dismal place, probably because it was perpetually dark and chilly, even through the summer. In the winter the coolie-type lampshade cast a sombre light which intensified the grey nooks and crannies. A constant damp, dank atmosphere added to my goose-pimpling fears, and made me shiver sometimes on a hot day, for of course no form of heating had ever warmed our shop, not even when the coldest winter days arrived.

Beside this lack of comfort, the refrigerated gloom was encouraged by the fact that the display windows had inside shutters. My father hated customers peering between the packages to his secret domain behind the shelves and counter. These wooden covers were continually almost closed — only the smallest chink of light was allowed to penetrate within. Thus, with all these reasons, for a number of years I would only dash through this dreary prison with hurried frightened steps.

I both hated and longed for the sound of the jangling doorbell that would occasionally shatter the usual stillness of our lives. That jarring noise warned and yet tantalised. Perhaps someone had come to steal away my father's attention from me, and how I resented the intrusion! On the other hand it could be that at last there was a rich buyer who would spend a lot of money and brighten my poor father's working day and set the till a-jingling.

When my quiet but concerned father was more withdrawn and silent than usual, sitting pained with his eyes closed, it meant he had a headache and mustn't be disturbed. If he was longer at the counter than the occasional customer warranted, it spelled out that his best buddy was with him and they would be talking for some time. The message was "Elizabeth, amuse yourself". These signs, and the resulting communication, were understood quite early on by his daughter, and as I grew I accepted the challenge.

Until formal education fostered playmates, and while my wise elderly companion was with his friend or nursing a migraine, the most wonderful thing for solitary entertainment was dipping into my mother's button tin. It sat on top of the sewing machine and, being a great one for making do and mending, she had kept all the fasteners cut from really worn out garments in this intriguing container. What an amazing treasure trove it turned out to be! Each time I dived into its depths, some very pretty and unusually shaped buttons, not seen before, would be fished out — there were so many in that enormous box. Today I still have the remnants of it. It was a good guessing game trying to remember from whose old clothes, recently discarded, this one or that one had been snipped. Perhaps it had been on Dad's very old cardigan, Mum's worn out working dress or my outgrown coat. My counting prowess was encouraged by sorting, matching and seeing how many there were in each set. It proved to be modern maths begun two or three generations too early. Several times I tried to find out exactly how many there were altogether but always forgot or muddled the final number — it was such a marathon task.

Suddenly, round about my fifth birthday, my attitude towards our business premises began to change. Newly discovered confidence and courage, learned from starting school, came to my aid. If my father was not available and the shop was empty, it became a wet-day playroom with all the varying bits and pieces which really encouraged imaginative games. It took on many differing locations depending on the stories read from my father's repertoire and the stimulation given by my teacher. In turn it was a deep unending cavern, a tiger's lair, a bear's den, home for a witch or dwarf, perhaps a castle, a cell or even a dungeon. Yet, until I left that background for good, it never quite lost its rather exciting, slightly foreboding, stomach-curdling feeling, which both excited and alarmed.

Brooding bays under partitioned shelves and creepy caves beneath the counter were a child's tingling pleasure. Empty boxes and discarded dummy packets from window-dressing proved to be highly imaginative and creative building materials once the real terror had been overcome. These were an unending source of thrills and enjoyment for a lonely friendless child because, sadly, no school associates or neighbours' children were allowed beyond the counter. Above the murky hideaways, jars of sweets stood sentinel. Daily, taste buds would be abortively tortured by viewing sherbet dips, brightly wrapped toffees, liquorice allsorts, swizzle sweets and aniseed balls. Below these on the counter were trays of tiger nuts, locust beans and sometimes honeycomb. These concoctions were the popular staple mouth-watering diet of the younger clientèle. The small stock of groceries held little play appeal in the early stages but the vinegar barrel often served as gun protection for an imaginary fortress, while bottles of lemonade, cream soda and sterilised milk frequently guarded an imprisoned princess.

Some seasons brought their own special excitements. The mounting anticipation leading to the Oxford and Cambridge boat race still remains in my memory. Clearly I can recall rummaging through old boxes for last year's emblems, hoping one at least would remain, and also wondering what shapes would be the current badge for the renowned river battle. Weekly halfpennies and coins, given occasionally by my father's cronies, would be carefully hoarded to enable me to wear my college's new favours. If I could sport an old as well as a new one, my schoolmates might be duly impressed, and sometimes I could buy an outdated one quite cheaply. Yet in recollection they all seemed to be furry animals, mostly curly-tailed monkeys. We never possessed a radio in the 1930s but our immediate neighbours always had theirs on very loudly, and on boat race day I was allowed out in the backyard to listen eagerly for the result. Even with colour television today and the race seen stage by stage, there is nothing now to compare with the thrill of the contest in those days. Cambridge blue was my favourite colour for many years.

One afternoon, towards the end of October, whilst listening to the quiet murmur of adult conversation as my father talked to one of his cronies, a most terrifying face suddenly leered across the counter at me. It seemed to have all the colours of flames and appeared alight, and that awful visage fixed me with its staring eyes from far back in its head. I screamed and screamed! I can still hear that hysterical screaming; I was beside myself. Then the demon gurgled, the adults laughed, but my father cuddled me, as a boy from up the street tore off his mask. November 5th never had the same appeal as the university boat race. Perhaps the cold foggy days of that particular month had something to do with it. Most of all, though, I suspect the real reason was that fire had always bothered me, even before our conflagration had occurred, and was certainly the cause of childish nightmares after our chimney had caught alight.

In our back room we had an old-fashioned kitchen range around which we sat in winter for warmth and cheer, as well as using it for cooking purposes. My father exerted tough elbow grease to polish it with Zebo blacking once a week, when he cleaned the place, taking great pains in its wonderful shine. On this one occasion he argued that my mother must have put some suet skin in the grate to increase the heat in the oven and so finish off her cakes. That she certainly sometimes did. Whatever started the blaze, the roar of the burning soot, seeing the flames thrusting out of the chimney pot, inhaling the insidious stench in our kitchen and feeling the heat permeating throughout the whole house were memories which continued to assault our senses for many months. From that very episode my bad dreams began, and unfortunately we never had a coal fire again. An uncomfortable evil-smelling oil stove remained our only means of winter warmth from then on and gave our home one of its unpleasant distinctive odours.

As the guys were burned on bonfires, and my father sold both their hideous masks and scary fireworks, I naturally linked these things with our disaster, and the dislike of that historic celebration increased until I was much older. Another cause of this almost paranoia was that during the approach to this particular time, live Jumping Jacks and Catherine Wheels (somehow it was always these two types) were often thrown alight into our shop, reviving fears for me of our chimney fire. Probably the unwelcome missiles had been purchased from us. Naturally I was not allowed to waste my low resources on such trash, as Father called it, nor was I unhappy about that fact.

Then, as now, Christmas was the highlight of the year. For a child living behind an unusually quiet counter, the sudden fervour and extra activity was intense and exciting. The smell of the place even changed. Gradually there was a certain whiff of interesting cardboard, the sickly inviting scent of fancy sweets, special party biscuits, candied peel, mixed dried fruits and extra-tempting chocolates. The customary sparsely filled, widely spaced jars were pushed closer together and added to, on festively prepared shelves, and all were filled to the very top.

Although my father didn't indulge in many decorations, what he did hang gave the shop a prettier, busier and more pleasing appearance — certainly for one small child. Then there was more work, more

16

action and many more customers in those first years in our backwater premises than at any other time of the calendar. Many large intriguing boxes had to be prised open and eagerly investigated, and there were lots of brightly wrapped packages needing to be stacked. It was wonderful to be involved. It made us the close family I wanted so badly. Everything was very tempting! How I longed to have lots of money to buy presents for those I loved, and some to spare for myself of course.

"If we eat all the profits, we'll never have a successful business," was Dad's favourite comment, and everything taken from the shop had to be paid for. We were rarely given anything from his stocks. Mother had to buy every bit of grocery from her hard-earned charring wages. How my dad provided cash for his own few cigarettes, which were usually cheap Woodbines, I often wondered. Any frugal pocket money had to be used to purchase my own sweets. The occasional halfpenny, when I was five, didn't go very far. That guiding rule certainly puzzled me, for although we always bought our requests and never did eat the profits without paying for them, we certainly didn't become rich — in fact it was the reverse, we became poorer and poorer. It just didn't work.

There were very exciting times, though, when new products came onto the market. My father seldom ventured into experimenting with fresh brands of varieties; however, I do remember several marvellous occasions when Mother and I acted as judge and jury. White Nestlé's bars were declared good on two counts:

the taste was very sweet and moreish, appealing to my childish appetite, and it had the blessing of being less messy than its brown counterpart. Once we shared a whole Mars bar . . . and didn't have to pay one penny for the sheer joy of tasting something quite yummy and most delicious. A Caley double-six packet was the last thing tested, and by me alone. An indulgent aunt also introduced me to the nectar of Aero chocolate, something my parents never stocked.

Playing shops was a very popular hobby as I grew older. The days gradually increased when my elderly father was unwell, worn down by stress and the 1930s Depression. The sweet-smelling gloom of the shop would tempt me to creep in and play with the shining golden scales while he rested in his chair. The graded brass weights were like thick golden coins, lovely to hold and touch, and in imagination made me feel quite rich. Great satisfaction came from exactly balancing them with sweets and little packages. My ambition was to grow tall enough and strong enough to lift the big display jars, then perhaps I might be allowed to serve the real customers. Conscientiously my father's skill in making cone-shaped newspaper bags had been copied, and I really longed to be left to cope on my own, trying out my knowledge.

During the school holidays there was a routine worked out by myself of self-appointed tasks to help my father. The doormat had to be banged on the concrete approach early every morning. Then the path had to be swept. Using the long-handled feather duster, the apprentice tradesman or tradeswoman flittered among the jars and packages. The lino floor was mopped over with a damp cloth and things on the counter were straightened. These were chores I really enjoyed when school was closed. Then it was good to pretend they were my own premises, and I would chat to imaginary customers as I had heard my father do. Yet when I was old enough to be a reliable assistant in the shop, contrariwise the desire had gone and I was a very reluctant helper.

I never really longed to be a grown-up shopkeeper when I was a child or teenager. Dislike, often truly bordering on hatred, would overwhelm me when school friends described outings with their mothers and fathers. They visited relations, had trips to the cinema, even pantomimes, with both parents — experiences never enjoyed by my whole family, and only rarely with even just my mother. We never went out all together, even to do ordinary shopping or take a short walk. The premises must never be closed until late every day, just in case a few delayed intending patrons might be missed. The shop was the ruling, dominating, evil influence of our lives and it made us different from other people, or so it appeared to me.

Once only can I remember my father joining my mother and me for a late afternoon stroll, and that instance was extended into the evening of George V and Queen Mary's Silver Jubilee celebrations. We walked about to see the street decorations in the early warm summer twilight. Holding both my parents' hands, whilst my mother pushed the pram with her unclaimed one, I skipped along the pavement between them with great pride and happiness, a day sadly never to be repeated. No! I never wanted to have my own shop, ever!

CHAPTER
THREE

The World Outside

Each venture is a new beginning.
T. S. Eliot

As many cats are reputed to have second homes where they often seek refuge, however caring their real owners may be, so from about the age of four I too found another retreat. It was very special, my own secret place, where I went all by myself and discovered companions of my own age and learned to do many exciting things. Just round the corner from the shop was an old grey stone edifice, with a lofty spire pointing people to God, called St Stephen's Church. Even today in a very different world, many years later, Sunday mornings still have an atmosphere all their own — silent, calm and restful — but then as a child it seemed more poignant to me, or may only be so in retrospect.

Anyway, savouring the quieter, slower and more peaceful surroundings, I'd be poised in my very best attire, ears cocked. Just before 11.00 a.m., the church bells would suddenly shatter the hushed stillness, then, like an arrow shot from the bow, my scurrying feet would resound along the pavement, clattering me in a straight line to the service. How my infant heart overflowed with sheer delight, singing the hymns and choruses in the company of other young people, my new-found friends. How wonderful it was to have discovered some friends with whom to share my joys!

Further along, in the next house-packed road, were St Stephen's Hall and various other church buildings, including a sort of kitchen. We did enjoy the chanting in the church, but the busy activities in these rooms were even more interesting and inviting to local children. In complete contrast with the drab and busy overcrowded surroundings where we lived, this was our heaven, paid for by short and quite pleasant appearances in church.

Adult attendance there was rather poorer, especially in the depressed 1930s, but the under-elevens put up a much better showing — no doubt because most of them were sent to that place, enabling distraught parents to have a Sunday respite. Certainly my father, and sometimes even my mother too, enjoyed a Sunday afternoon nap as customers seldom intruded until after teatime. So I also was encouraged to seek out those other church premises. Moreover, we children continued to come regularly, thanks to the great dedication and lively ideas maintained by three kindly teachers, all unmarried, with sufficient income releasing them to devote much time to the needy young of the district. I hated to be absent, even if unwell, in case a new project might be missed.

Attractive pictorial stamps were distributed weekly depicting well-known Bible stories, which we lapped up eagerly and stuck proudly in the allotted spaces of a book provided. Other bonuses were really bright crayons (we never had such brilliant ones at home), interesting printed pictures to colour, and we were constantly encouraged to make up our own little plays based on the parables that had been explained so interestingly to us. This particularly appealed to me, and when I was about seven stimulated me to write them down. Any bit of scrap paper was seized upon to record my jottings. One parent thought for a while that he had a budding genius on his hands; Mother said it was a waste of paper, but she laughed kindly and ruffled my hair.

"Elizabeth thinks she lives at church," my fond father used to say as I hopped up and down impatiently declaring that I couldn't wait for that special day to come round each week — he was so pleased with my enthusiasm and progress. Our young memories were certainly taxed. Many of us could recite speedily all the books of the Bible in the correct order and knew word-perfect a number of well-known texts. Our stamp books were nearly always very full by each December, when rewards for good attendance were distributed . . . we all received prizes because we all attended regularly.

The Christmas season was the highlight of the year, and how excitement mounted as the time drew near. Lines and readings had to be practised for the carol services. Manfully I also learned my party pieces, wanting to do them, yet fearing that under pressure the words would be forgotten. We'd wonder what games we'd play, and, best of all, anticipate the delicious tea, far more mouth-watering than any we had at home, with more of it and a much greater variety too.

Then there were the rather impatient (on my part) fittings, and the making of the new dress. My very understanding mother, who liked to make her little daughter look pretty, always seemed to manage in those earlier years to persuade my rather reluctant father to let me have a party frock. Miraculously she would look out a very cheap remnant from the local drapers, and, in spite of always being overworked, cleverly run up an attractive outfit with tremendous speed. For one prancing, jigging child, though, it never seemed quick enough. When it was at last hanging on the bedroom door "my cup just overflowed"! Now the party was bound to be perfect.

The strange thing is that I remember more about the dress I never did wear for any of my special events than I do of the ones I actually used for several important occasions before they became everyday wear. When I was seven plus, and what proved to be the last really happy carefree Christmas in our home before the war was declared, my dear mum produced an even more beautiful garment than usual. I remember it clearly. The background was pale yellow, with little sprigs of summer posies dotted about the material. It had little puffed sleeves, a Peter Pan collar and wide matching sash. The fully gathered skirt flared out beautifully when I twisted round like most small girls loved to do. High drama struck a few days before the event. The signs of a slight cold persuaded my over-anxious father to state firmly, ever careful to protect his only chick,

"Your woollen dress will be warmer, otherwise the party is off! We don't want you to be ill and miss school afterwards." There was no arguing or moving him in this mood so, rather than be absent from the longed-for celebrations, I sadly bowed to the inevitable.

Visits to portrait studios were not customary then for folks in our circumstances, but a very reasonable photographer, by happy chance, took a room in our church and must have been exceedingly cheap as many of us Sunday School children, including yours truly, had appointments. The fates were again contrary, and it proved to be the type of day when the very biting wind forecasts future snow. So there was a further ban on the lovely outfit, and the very itchy woolly one had to suffice once more or no picture.

The twice-thwarted yellow creation was safely hung in the cupboard for summer wearing. Then, to cap it all, that spring I put on an unexpected spurt and outgrew my strength — as the term goes. The bodice was too tight, the skirt too short and there hadn't been enough material for the deep hem my mother usually favoured. However, with her customary ingenuity, she rose to the occasion once more and with extra contrasting material altered the dress into one suitable for school. For me, though, it never had the same appeal, but I had to wear it, and it seemed then to fit me for ages in its second, more mundane state.

Now, to return to the parties and performances: regardless of the dress, the festivities were frequently almost missed, yet never quite, because of feeling sick with anticipation. That year tears of frustration and self-pity about the frock aggravated things. Yet, when it came to the day, as usual I found it very stimulating to prove I could be word-perfect and gain approval from the adults and my contemporaries with my party pieces. It was a shame that on this one occasion I almost spoiled my platform début, either because of tremendous relief or just carelessness, but whatever it was, full of pride during the clapping, I quickly turned and promptly fell off the stage, which almost drowned the loud sympathetic applause with even louder uncontrolled wailing. "How, indeed, are the mighty fallen!"

One Sunday morning before I was eight, Miss Tintsel said unequivocally and very definitely, "God says we must not shop on his day. We must keep the Sabbath Day holy. It is His day and for rest. He commands us to rest too." The hall floor almost moved from underneath me and I'm sure I flushed a most guilty red. Not only did both my parents at some time take from the business and pay for packets they required on Sunday; what was even more serious and damning, to a mere seven-year-old, my father even opened his premises for business and absolutely broke God's law. As I was their daughter, I thought the guilt was also mine by virtue of living with them. Then it dawned rather reluctantly on me that I had spent a penny a few months before when Uncle Charlie visited us and that had been a Sunday too. So I was well and truly involved on my own account. We must all be very wicked! How would any one of us get to heaven when we died? It made me very sorrowful and frightened, especially on my poor father's behalf. He seemed doubly implicated.

For a very long time I simply hoped there would be no more Sunday customers, as much as we desperately needed them and their money. Also I wished my parents would get their necessary packages on Saturday. With bated breath I anxiously awaited each week's topic and story, hoping that particular one was finished and done with, and that Miss Tintsel wouldn't question me on the subject. Of course, being a very quiet child and avoiding trouble if possible, I didn't mention the problem to anyone, least of all to my parents. I loved them so much and didn't want to think they were bad, neither did I want to stop going to St Stephen's which, apart from that difficulty, was heaven itself to me. What a predicament! And how I was divided in my loyalties! Like most sinners I hoped it would just go away, and for a while it did, but it gave me a very hard time, and constant nightmares were the result.

Gradually things quietened down, months and years passed and my life in Sunday School widened. The pleasant summer outings to the vicar's garden extended to a coach trip (my very first), right into Epping Forest. Then there was an excursion to the sea, to Southend in fact. Although I had already been there by train one wonderful day with my mother and her friend, it had been such a lovely treat it bore repetition as a Sunday School outing. Finally, there came a marvellous boat trip to Clacton.

As we became juniors, the Christmas activities included proper nativity plays performed in church before family and friends, in my case in front of one parent, my mother. It was wonderful to graduate from a shepherd to an angel, and then, joy of joys, to Mary's part. These little productions gave us all confidence and aroused in me a keenness and real love for drama which has lasted all my life.

It was with splendid fervour that I joined the Band of Hope when I was in the junior section. Not much was really known by me about that organisation, but the Sunday School teachers were ardent supporters and it was very easy to become a member. Also, in my muddled mind, adhering seemed to atone somewhat for breaking the Sabbath Day commandment and this time there was no conflict with my home life.

My parents considered themselves too poor to take alcohol, and were considerably concerned about the manner in which my maternal grandmother wasted what little pension she had in buying jugs of stout. Much later I discovered that they did not object to someone treating them to just one drink. Anyway, with particular zeal and zest to help my wayward grandmother, I proceeded to fight the demon drink. There proved to be lots of interesting stories, discussions, tests, competitions and rewards to spur on keen supporters of the Band of Hope. Each year enthusiasm to excel urged me on to sit examinations under the temperance auspices. Just before the war began, I was awarded first place in the Chelmsford Diocese and eventually top marks in all England, and I received the complete works of Shakespeare which, furthermore, helped my school work.

There were also singing competitions. Once my partner and I won a duet contest but these ordeals were worrying, especially when the advice given was, "Take a raw egg whipped in milk to clear the throat." Following that precept revolted me; I was sick, nearly missed the competition and finally decided that vocally it was not my cup of tea, even though it obviously did the trick and we were awarded certificates. Eventually Mother was disappointed that I wasn't following in her footsteps with singing skills, but in my general love of drama I was certainly her daughter.

Now, with hindsight, my heartfelt thanks go out to all those generous willing people who did so much to bring some knowledge to deprived young city urchins and who filled their drab lives so devotedly with interesting activities and red-letter days. From them we also gained a great love of the Bible and it paved the way for me to become a Christian later in my life. That quotation from Proverbs proved correct in my case, "Train up a child in the way he should go, and when he is old he will not depart from it." The real truths I learned there never left me and, even in spite of the problem of Sunday opening and later the evils of gambling, I never wanted to leave the church, my secret and happy retreat.

Three months after reaching the age of five, the local council school took charge of my general education. How both exciting and rather scary was that very first day — even my impoverished father had a great sense of occasion and must have been concerned for his daughter. He actually shut the shop for a whole hour that Monday morning in order to introduce me to the next big step in my life. As usual, my poor mother was working. Looking back, her whole life seemed to be taken up with work — it must have been very hard for her.

My word! The playground was absolutely full of noisy children, so many more than every Sunday at St Stephen's. Yet gripping my father's hand, feeling so proud and pleased he was with me, we advanced to the big entrance hall. After all the particulars were settled we were directed to the beginners' class. When I realised that my father had gone, I remember rushing to the closed door to follow him, but I couldn't reach the high handle sufficiently well to turn it, so any escape was thwarted. I must have soon settled.

Blackboard and chalk were not new to me, but, although I was able to have a good attempt at my name, fright made me forget on that day. To quieten my fears I was given plasticine — I have never liked that smelly material since. However, drill, running, jumping and skipping in the playground, in disciplined conditions, delighted me. Confidence grew as the colouring experience from Sunday School proved my skill here also. The story at the end of the day must have been gripping because Dad said I wanted so much to return next morning that I gladly left him and, holding the hand of a big girl next door, launched off on my own.

The lavatories caused the first and only real problem I can recollect in the Primary department and brought me up against the teacher's authority quite early in my school days. Our privy at home was along the cement yard and round the corner. It was always dark, with the door closed, and it was one of my tasks to tear up the newspaper used there for necessary cleaning purposes. Although the school toilets were very similar and even had proper toilet paper and, moreover, in themselves weren't upsetting, shyness with all those children pushing in at playtime and having a strong healthy bladder, I avoided using them in those early days.

Actually, it was almost impossible for small new pupils to run the gauntlet of the hordes barricading that area at playtime. The class teacher must have known this and tried to help her scholars, because only a few days after the term had begun she asked, when break had ended, "Who hasn't used the lavatories this lunch time?" Feeling very embarrassed and nervous, but always honest, slowly my hand went up with several others. We were immediately sent back into the yard to remedy our omission. As there were still quite a few of us children and I didn't need to go, again I just stayed outside and returned with the obedient ones. Yes, you guessed, someone sneaked on me! Out I had to go once more with the teacher's cross words ringing in my ears and tears welling up into my eyes. Beaten, metaphorically speaking, and escorted by my informant and, except for her, all alone in the lavatory, I felt it best to conform. I never went again, though, to the school loos until I stayed for school dinners and, fortunately, there was no repetition of that question.

My mother had little spare time to help with any problems or questions to do with learning but encouraged me whenever I did well. It was my lonely, unoccupied father who supported and assisted with difficult sums, writing and reading problems, and letter formation. It seemed to give him real pleasure to sit down and explain puzzling processes to a confused child. Looking back now I realise he would have been a very good teacher, and I remember with real joy how rarely he lost patience when I was tired or extra dense. It was not until his health broke down and worries caused by the Depression began to bite that he got impatient and cross with his growing pupil.

Reading did not come easily in spite of my father's help. The first teacher in the Junior department had a quite noisy bad temper and shouted at us if we hesitated and halted when speaking out in class. This frightened me and made for loss of concentration when reading, and my voice became softer and softer which annoyed her. "You are definitely one of my bad readers," was her verdict, and those damning words sank deep into my brain, but their unfairness stirred me into action. Dad responded quickly to pleas for help, and he heard me read before as well as after school each day. For my part, in my own bedroom, I'd practise aloud in front of the mirror, looking up occasionally, imagining Mrs McDonald watching and listening, and perhaps shouting at me, thereby helping me to improve my reading skills. By the end of that school year I was one of the top group in the class for all types of English and for sums. So perhaps, after all, she did me a lot of good.

Being seven was an important milestone — I was allowed then to do many things like shopping, going to church in the evening and going to school all alone. It made me feel very grown up and important; however it soon occurred to me that independence brings responsibilities and worries. Crossing a rather busy road (by those long-ago standards) near the school seemed so easy with the big girl from next door shepherding me over, but having to decide myself, when to cross, and when to weave in and out of parked cars was quite different. Pride again stopped me from speaking of the difficulty. Each day I plotted to arrive at the kerb at about the same time as someone else. The number of times my buckle, shoelace or button supposedly came undone was amazing as I waited for them to catch up. When the others were ready, then I'd pop up and walk just behind them over the street. Gradually I braved it alone and finally took it all in my stride.

Now a greater agony for me, and a more prolonged burden I just dare not explain to my parents as I thought it would worry them, was how I managed to lose many small articles of clothing so frequently. After a while some of the bigger boys in the Junior School began to realise that I lived in a sweet shop and they tried to blackmail me. As I left the school gates, either a scarf, hat, pair of gloves, handkerchief or hair slide would be snatched and as they ran off a short distance they yelled to me to get them some sweets, and then they would give back the stolen articles. Constant hot water overwhelmed me, figuratively, when I timidly confessed to forgetting or mislaying these stolen belongings. My mother and father began to think I was stupid or very careless, and finally were extremely cross about the cost of replacing them. It was a very traumatic period and seemed to last for an eternity.

Slowly my tormentors grasped the fact that it was a fruitless task. How could they understand it wasn't all a bed of roses living in a confectioner's shop, especially when the very few treats permitted had to be paid for by raiding my own, always very slender, money-box? Eventually even their great tenacity slackened and they lost interest in harassing me. During that awful era, how I longed to be able to acquiesce in their demands, yet had I been able to do so, there might not have been so early a reprieve. Sadly my limited experience with bullying hadn't extended that far then, but I was learning fast.

Apart from the occasional aggression from one's peers, it was usually safe, even in our part of London, to let young children go to and return from school unaccompanied by adults when the hours of daylight were short. Errands were run, and even church meetings were attended in the dark, dashing from lamp post to lamp post whilst singing at the top of my voice, so as to keep up my spirits; no adults then whisked their offspring by car to evening activities or social occasions. My confidence and courage grew in leaps and bounds — friendly, sociable and boastful fitted my general description.

"We've a new girl coming to our class this morning. Who will make her feel at home and tell her what we do in class six?" asked Miss Meade, who was my next teacher. "Please, Miss, I will," was my prompt reply. It was a sunny warm day and I remember thinking how nice and pretty Winnie looked. We smiled shyly at each other as she sat down beside me. That day was the beginning of our long friendship. How pleased I was to take Winnie round the playground and tell her all about our school. It wasn't long before she introduced her six-year-old sister who was attending my old Infant department. Doreen looked at us through the railings and immediately I knew she was a "funny" girl, what my parents described as "mentally deficient", but there was a sort of appeal about her, and because I liked Winnie and wanted her friendship I grew to like Doreen.

The baker called at our shop, but my parents never used the milkman's services as we sold that awful liquid called sterilised milk. Luckily I drank cold water. Most of our groceries were bought from our shop too, but there were still vegetables, occasionally fruit, and even less frequently meat to be purchased elsewhere. In between her many chores, my mother went to the shopping centre which took its name, the Baker's Arms, from a well-known local public house — and I often went with her. After my seventh birthday it became my job to get ordinary and essential goods, but fruit and meat were too expensive and dodgy to leave to such inexpert selection.

Going to Sainsbury's in those days was a pleasure to me — I loved the delicious lingering smells of savoury foods, the pristine gleam of clean tiled walls and constantly sponged counters. For the first few times the shopping always took me longer than my parents estimated. I was fascinated to watch the assistants, whose skill serving the butter in oblongs with patterned, wooden battens was very time-consuming. They did it so neatly and uniformly. It always amazed me how clever the servers were at guessing the correct amount, invariably at the first attempt.

Hinton's, the local draper, was another time-wasting store. It seemed an exceedingly big store with several interesting departments, and how cleverly they tossed the chosen bales of material! In my mind I sorted out what remnant I hoped my mother would be able to buy next. It was interesting to see the assistants measuring out the pretty stuff along the fixed metal rule, and I wondered if they ever made mistakes when they took the plunge with the scissors and actually cut the piece right off. Overhead was an even more fascinating gadget, a sort of railway along which travelled little tubs. It was amazing to hand money over for a purchase, watch the assistant pop the bill and pennies into a container, fit it into the tube, then pull a handle attached to a cord that sent the whole lot bouncing along the overhead wires to the cash desk. There it was checked, the necessary change inserted in the tube, and the whole procedure reversed, causing the money to come bobbing back along the line. I never knew it to take the wrong rails or to crash into any other tub, but it always concerned me that it might. Many trips were made to the haberdashers for cottons, darning wool, needles and tapes as my mother was always making do and mending, so I frequently saw this marvellous device at work. But the best outings with her were when odd lengths for a new dress were on the list.

Our most exciting joint shopping sprees, and then only very very occasional ones, took place on Saturday evenings. We both went hoping to acquire some perishable foods being sold cheaply to avoid uncertain weekend storage — the days of general refrigeration were yet to come. It would be for a rare Sunday treat — a roast dinner. Besides a reasonable small joint, we looked for reduced vegetables. It made my heart leap when I heard the verbal invitation, "Coming to the High Street with me, Elizabeth?" "Course, Mum," would be the prompt reply and I'd rush to get our coats. We'd walk along companionably through a maze of narrow streets and back ways in the opposite direction to the Baker's Arms. Perhaps there would be an extra treat for me as well?

This centre was a large, mainly Jewish shopping area with, I remember, mostly proper dress shops along both sides of the long straight street. In the gutters were stalls full of very reasonable merchandise. Always it was very crowded and noisy, with vendors shouting out their prices and cracking funny jokes. It was both exciting and disturbing for a small child, and we tightly grasped each other's hand. Probably the strange smell and shadowy flickering of the kerosene lamps hanging on the wooden supports of the covered counters intensified the mysterious atmosphere. Shop owners would come out of their smarter premises should you stop, or even slightly hesitate, glancing at their window displays. They would come right up to would-be buyers, but were never aggressive or unpleasant. Wanting customers, they could be wheedling and persistent, but never difficult. Although my mother never succumbed, I was always fearful they might just persuade her. She did love pretty things and then what would Daddy say?

Always busy and hectic, it was even more so on dark winter evenings and really exciting as Christmas drew near. The stalls would be extra full and most attractively displayed, the shops brighter and more gaily decorated. Until my eighth birthday, we always had a few special delights in the festive season, especially if we bought them at the cheaper end of the day. How clever my mother was to buy little stocking fillers whilst I was with her, without me really knowing until the proper occasion, and then I thought Father Christmas had brought them.

Whatever the time of the year, she would often surprise me with a little package of sweets or a fancy cake (all to be eaten before we returned). Perhaps best of all was that nectar of the gods, a drink of sarsaparilla. Although never actually forbidden, I knew better than even to hint about our indulgences to my father. Yet I could always square my overworked conscience to accept that it wasn't really very deceitful — my love of treats was always stronger than my weaker sense of guilt.

The seemingly longer walk home with quite heavy bags for both of us didn't spoil the lovely day. Yet to come was the weekly bath by the fire in the scullery, summer or winter. Before we had even started out, Dad had filled the old-fashioned brick corner copper that needed whitening every week to keep it looking good. Then he would have lit the fire underneath, so that the water would be boiling when we returned. By then, too, the old oil cloth would have been put under one of the several tin baths unhooked from the yard fence, placed near the boiler fire ready for the major bathing operation, beginning with the youngest.

My parents' anticipation and enjoyment, I sensed, did not match mine. It must have required a lot of heavy work on their part and was a long drawn-out ritual. Sitting by my father whilst Mum had her turn, my wet hair would be rubbed so soothingly. On such a night in those early days there was always a special supper treat, which we would have persuaded him was very cheap, and as I tucked in he would tell me my usual bedtime story, but somehow it sounded better on bath nights. It was a perfect ending to the occasional perfect day.

CHAPTER
FOUR

The Extended Family and Neighbours

All happy families resemble one another, but each unhappy family is unhappy in its own way.

Tolstoy from *Anna Karenina*

There is a saying, a very true one I've discovered with growing maturity, that suggests how to keep dealings with blood relations sweet: "Put your hearts together but pitch your tents apart." That certainly applied to the Pritchards and the Cronks. During the 1930s travelling was not that easy for any of us, and our small branch of the family was particularly poor. This general lack of money didn't encourage intercourse even though the actual mileage between a number of us wasn't that excessive; so the costs, and often lack of spare time, kept kith and kin apart. Yet thankfully, at least as far as I was concerned, there was sufficient communication to stimulate some relationships. From quite an early age I bombarded my father with requests for stories about the family. It was good to feel that I belonged, and probably because I was an only child for eight years I desperately wanted to know about my roots.

In spite of my father's co-operation it was my mother's relations who featured most in those early years. She had an elder sister, twelve years her senior (their only brother, who came between them chronologically, died in his teens), who lived in Rainham, Essex, with her considerable quiver of children. Aunt Alice must have left home when Mother was about six, but from Mum's snatches of information, I understand that they used to meet together fairly frequently until she married much later and moved to Walthamstow. Yet until a couple of years before the war there were no meetings between our two families.

The Rainham sister's casual way of life and standards of childcare didn't meet with her brother-in-law's approval and he didn't like to mix with us. To be fair, the age gap and elder girl's early marriage couldn't have fostered family ties either. Anyway, according to my father's judgement, they were a feckless bunch, often drunk, dirty and badly fed, and the parents frequently left their progeny unsupervised. Poor Dad, how did he feel a few years later when, due to economic pressure and ill health, one or two of these sad descriptions applied to his own family and home? Once a rather noisy altercation about these relations, which just couldn't help being overheard, ended very unhappily with one parent shouting most angrily and the other once more shrinking into his shell, silent and moody for many days. Of course we didn't make a visit then, or at any other time after, for many years to that aunt.

Auntie Ethel and Uncle Charlie were quite another proposition. Although also true cockneys, like all Mother's family, they were more warmly welcomed by my parents. She was Mother's younger sister and Charlie her future husband. They enjoyed going to pubs, parties and music halls, yet they were always pleasant to my quiet, studious father and did not press my parents to do as they did. They came to visit us several times before they were married and spoiled their niece considerably. There was sometimes a surprise at the bottom of my bed the morning after they had paid a rather late visit to the shop. Mother was always talking about her sister Ethel, yet there is no memory of any of us going to their actual wedding. There was a consistent closeness between these two sisters, and as I grew I too understood that they were very fond of each other. Mum always sang in our house on the red-letter days when they were meeting each other, and although we went to them more often than they came to us, Dad seldom seemed to mind sparing money for our fares.

However, we usually had to get his permission first before planning our trips to Deptford, but then what joy! Mum and I would run to the station and catch a train to the murky echoing Liverpool Street station. Once accustomed to the dirt and noise, how I loved the whistling clatter and the foggy sizzling steam. Even the smuts that got on my best clothes and the dirt on my usually unsoiled hands, which, unsuccessfully, I always tried to hide, added to the thrill of the adventure.

We would start at Hoe Street Station, and puffing and jolting through Hackney we'd both screw up our noses and pull out our hankies to stem the really revolting smell which poured forth from the Yardley factory nearby. It was so difficult to associate that awful stench with the beautiful lavender perfume my mother had received once as a birthday gift from her unmarried friend Mary. As a special treat when going on our infrequent travels, a spot would be rubbed behind my ears, so I knew that scent from certain experience.

Looking at the tiny back gardens and right into some dwellings, almost beside the railway lines with hardly any yard at all, made me feel so pleased and grateful that we had a really large patch, all 40 feet of it, behind our shop where I could play on warm sunny days. I considered myself very fortunate then.

We'd hurry, laughing and shouting above the echoing clashing of carriages and engines, through the musty sooty terminus to the bus, which was nearly always waiting outside. It delivered us right to the top of Grandma's road. Newly-married Auntie and her husband had two rooms in her mother's house, so we could kill two birds with one stone, so to speak.

Suddenly the pleasure of our journey would dim, familiar landmarks would be noted from the top of the vehicle, and every time we neared Rolt Street feelings of panic would rise up within me. Tugging at Mother's arm, I'd urgently whisper, "Don't stop at the vinegar

shop, Mummy! Please don't stop at the vinegar shop!"
A strange request, no doubt you are thinking? It was
the custom to see if Grandma and her brother Uncle
Tom were inside The Queen's Head public house, just
where we alighted from the bus — they usually were.
My heart would sink; that would necessitate a long wait
while they were found and bought a drink by their
younger visiting relative, my mum. Even now, all these
years later, I can smell that curdling, retching odour
and recall how my chest throbbed and my stomach
ached. It was a real workman's city pub, which had a
much stronger stench lingering outside the building,
and yet the odour was slightly akin to that around our
vinegar barrel in our premises. That was the association
for me and ours was bad enough, but The Queen's
Head smell was more sour, much staler and more
revoltingly unsavoury, which caused me to tremble and
heave, longing for my parent to return. One day I was
properly sick. It was my salvation. From then on I was
allowed to run down the road to Grandma's house
while Mum performed her filial duty and so I escaped
the one dreadful drawback to our lovely treat.

Grandma Pritchard was always a shadowy, almost
unknown personality, more so than my father's dead
parents about whom he was often telling me interesting
snippets. My maternal grandmother sat fairly upright in
her armchair — a large, fat, always a sedentary figure,
apart from her pilgrimage to and from her drinking
mecca at the top of the road. Her hair gathered back
into a bun, she reminded me, as I learned more history,
of Queen Victoria. Like her, she always wore a black

dress with a grey shawl or cardigan round her shoulders, and long black boots which I sometimes helped to unbutton. Kissing her was expected, but not really relished by her, nor was it spontaneous on my part, and gradually I realised the reason for my abhorrence. Around her, like The Queen's Head, there was an unwholesome vinegary pungency which increased my shyness and repelled me. Even more slowly, I began to understand that my grandmother, besides being a heavy drinker, was incontinent as well. Poor lady, and poor Auntie Ethel too.

After a colourless "Hullo" when she did arrive at home from The Queen's Head, no other words were exchanged between us until "Bye-bye" when we left, and no doubt we both said it with considerable relief. It never improved. It began to dawn on me also that her daughters didn't want to encourage her drinking habit, but it was expected of them and the bad custom was continued. Sadly, she had no other interests, no domestic skills and no friends. How could Auntie Ethel and Uncle Charlie manage living under the same roof? I often puzzled about this and decided it was a good thing that we lived as far away as we did, but of course it meant that we didn't see Auntie and Uncle as much as I'd like. How contrary life can be!

Uncle Tom was Grandma's bachelor brother, and he also had a bedroom in her house and, as far as I could see, did more of the housework and housekeeping than she did. He was certainly a drinking partner sometimes, but he had a very new and gripping hobby which needed subsidising and so prevented him matching her intake of liquor. He possessed a wonderful magic box, and was more often sitting in his sister's kitchen, earphones on his head and a far away look in his eyes. My bottled-up expectancy was occasionally satisfied. Joy of joys! Sometimes he would ask if I'd like to listen. Perched on a footstool and with a great sense of wonder, I'd hear the fuzzy music and crackly talking on his magic crystal set. Fancy all that mysterious sound just coming out of the air into that special box! Later he became a fanatic with his wireless too; many times I would volunteer to fetch his heavy accumulator that worked this mysterious contraption. "We are the Ovaltineys Little Girls and Boys" was the pop song of later days, and I loved to sing it at home and was very proud to do so at school. It was a mark of great prestige and helped me to keep up with my classmates, several of whom actually had sets like my uncle's in their homes too.

Much earlier on in my visits to Deptford I was just in time to witness the local custom of the "cat's meat man" going on his rounds. He never called in our part of London, not that I remember anyway, but in Grandma's area he was a common sight. He was a little man in a cap, a roomy butcher's-type apron enveloping him, and he carried a tray of none-too-fresh strips of meat spiked onto rough skewers. As he trotted down the streets it was funny to see the gourmand cats prancing along behind him, and those in front, suddenly just relishing the interesting scent coming from their "pied piper", all turned round ready to be his vanguard, their tails held aloft, and ears pricked and noses twitching. He called at each customer's house and tucked the tasty tit-bits under their high door-knockers if they were absent. Those very interested felines weren't to be trusted.

Gradually Auntie Ethel had to do more for her ageing mother — she and Uncle Charlie took over the official rent book. Grandma just had her bedroom, and they looked after her and Uncle Tom, although he retained more independence than she did for far longer. I loved my namesake. She was a warm and cuddly person in those days, especially before she had her own family. Auntie and Uncle were my godparents, but when invited to be so I learned that they set one dire condition. That was that I should be named after her. Like most children do at some time, I have always hated my first Christian name, mostly because the nasty sneak in the then current popular girls' school stories was usually called Ethel. Much later I learned that my aunt's second name was Matilda — so perhaps I was fortunate after all!

Apart from really enjoying an occasional day out together in South London, Mother and I looked forward to Auntie's cooking. There was always lots of creamy milk and plenty of tasty meat in her meals, which were lacking in every one of ours. An enormous steak and kidney pudding or pie with delicious gravy and plenty of fresh green vegetables followed by rich, sweet rice pudding topped by a well-browned crunchy crisp skin was the most popular menu. Their usually well-hidden cats, already well served by the cat's meat man, put in a regular sudden appearance each dinnertime and did justice to any little portion, however small, that might be left behind.

There were two cats forever sitting snug in their sitting room, and as close to the fire inside the fender as was safe, in the winter. On warm summer days both would seek coolness under the cupboards in the constantly dark, shaded kitchen. These fat fluffy cats, with beautiful shiny fur, except if scorched by the fire during colder days, were named to indicate Uncle's drinking tastes — Brandy and Whisky, followed by Blackie and Whitey. Later cats reflected my aunt's patriotic streak, being called Queenie and Prince, changed later to Monty and Winnie. All their pets loved chocolate, often differing over the dark or white variety. This was particularly suitable as by that time my aunt and uncle lived in a sweet shop too.

Being a big, stockily built man with well-developed muscles and great strength, Uncle Charlie was often in rough clothes, and his language was loud and rough to match; these characteristics indicated Uncle's type of job. He was a stevedore at the Surrey Docks, but during the 1930s was more out of work than in, yet they never seemed to be poor as we were, and, once married, Auntie never had to help out with their income, as my poor mother always had to do by charring to support us and our shop. It did seem strange to their niece that, even with unemployment, they always had plenty of good food, quite nice clothes, and treats were still possible. They also continued to be very generous to their godchild. Subsequently I found out that Uncle was able to work for a relative who owned a thriving business in the dock area, and later that marvellous gold mine became his own little shop and provided them with an extremely good living for many years after the war.

Because of his type of work, it seemed to be a foregone conclusion that Uncle Charlie was the dominant partner, the boss in their partnership, and Auntie meekly fell in with his needs and suggestions. She always got up very early to prepare and cook his breakfast, while his dinner was always on the table exactly at the time he demanded with no exceptions made for unexpected delays. Many nights he left her alone to go out with his mates, pub drinking, gambling, or to the dogs. Yet he did look after her in his way. Occasionally he treated her to the Music Hall or a visit to the Hackney Empire and, if his flutters were successful and sometimes they were, he bought her lovely rings, necklaces, nice coats and shoes. Even when he left her by herself at nights, he would give her chocolates and her favourite orange drink. She was very grateful for any little considerations and for his ready money for food and the household needs.

Auntie never complained about her husband's rough language and sometimes rougher treatment when he was drunk, which was only very infrequent but most distressing on the occasions when it occurred. She was ever-loyal and told no-one except her sister, and inadvertently her quiet but ever-listening niece. Sadly, because of the life they lived, they grew very fat as they aged and had many resulting health problems.

To celebrate my fifth birthday Mum, bless her, took me to see the folks at Deptford. She knew how much we both loved the journey and spending time with her sister and brother-in-law. Excitement mounted as present time came round. My! It looked a most interesting cardboard box and so very high, the biggest gift ever . . . and my godparents had given it to me. As I held it gingerly, something moved inside. Oh! Was that a meow? Could it be? No, it couldn't! Then Auntie opened the top and a small furry head popped up and it looked at me. "It's a kitten, a little kitten, is it mine?" I shrieked almost disbelievingly. Those words still come to mind as I recall receiving the nicest present ever from my godparents, because by their smiling, nodding faces the earnest question was answered. It just had to be mine; I fondled its warm little body snuggling against mine, and love for it flowed through my very being.

Blackie was a very tiny black cat, so what else could we call him? With three little white paws and one speckly one, and a white smudge on his forehead, he was otherwise all black and his name suited him perfectly. At first Father wasn't too pleased to see an addition to our household — it was someone else to feed, and even I knew we had to be careful. So would he let me keep him? Also Dad wasn't an animal lover; I realise that now, but when he saw how delighted his little daughter was and how I continued to care for Blackie myself, he softened and really came to like my new friend.

Blackie proved to be a most placid affectionate pet and very tolerant of his young mistress's excessive display of devotion. He was nursed, cuddled and talked to constantly. School soon began to feature much more in my life now and as we played my furry friend would sit patiently (most times) on the low nursing chair in Miss Cronk's class, slate and chalk strategically beside him. Dressed in doll's clothes, he would stoically allow me to place him in the blanketed clothes basket which became his cot in our duet game of "Mothers and Fathers".

After eighteen very happy months of great companionship, Blackie suddenly became quite ill and had to be put to sleep. How I cried and cried! My parents vowed our Irish neighbours, with whom they had constant altercations, were responsible and had poisoned him. Mother said that Blackie would keep scratching in their immaculate garden. I only know that I was very bereft and achingly missed my gentle furry playmate.

The postman rarely came to our premises with private letters, only bills and business matters. Auntie Lily, Father's one sister, was the only fairly regular correspondent, writing twice a year, and she hadn't seen me since she dropped me as a baby, according to her brother's sad tale. Mother's family didn't seem to write at all — they just popped in to see us, and we did the same to them and rarely notified them of our coming.

One morning, during the school holiday, we had a brief postcard postmarked "Deptford". Mother was extremely excited and snatched it eagerly from my father's hand. She seemed very thrilled by what she read but said nothing to her daughter about the news it contained; she told me to hurry and get myself ready to go to see Grandma, and just whisked me off at breakneck speed on a surprise trip to Rolt Street. What is more, this time Dad didn't even make a little quibble about us going. There was an air of "you don't know what I know" about my female parent, and I sensed something quite important was in the offing and became highly curious and full of happy anticipation.

Imagine my absolute amazement when we arrived at Auntie's house; there was a pram outside — a real baby's pram, with a real wee baby tucked up cosily inside. Auntie Ethel had had a sweet little girl called Joan, and she was my cousin. After inspecting her little toes and fingers, and marvelling how tiny she was, my brain began to function, and counting rapidly I worked out that she was almost six years younger than me. Her arrival now made our rare journeys to Rolt Street even more desirable.

That first day my godmother let me proudly push Joan's pram when we took her to the local park. Yes, there was an additional pull to visit South London. Also it started me off on my favourite theme. Since I was about four I frequently requested, "Please may I have a little sister?" Now it was, "Please may I have a little sister like Joan? I'd help you look after her, Mummy, because I know how to — I watched Auntie." This plea was always side-tracked, and more often flatly refused by my parents. "Babies cost a lot of money and we can't afford one," was my father's standard reply.

Until I was nearly eight my small bed was in my parents' bedroom. Occasionally, after I was five, when there was no lodger in the spare room, I really enjoyed being in there on my own in the big double bed. It was sheer luxury to sink into the soft feather mattress with all the other bits and pieces around which had come from my paternal grandparents' home in Godalming. I loved to think of their granddaughter sleeping where they had slept long before I was born. Near the small sash window was their deep chest of drawers which, with a mirror on it, helped to serve as a dressing table. Another matching stack of drawers was beside the bed near the big built-in cupboard holding spare clothes and bedding, and finally two wooden Windsor chairs completed the furnishing.

Once I was a proper schoolgirl and gained confidence, I longed to have my very own room and refuge in the house. Above the fireplace, not far from the end of the bed, was just one picture, the only one in the place except for a text from the Bible printed on cardboard with the words "God so loved the world". That one picture, however, made a real impression on me from the very first time of being on my own in the spare room. If I woke early and it was cold but light I'd look at it intently from under the bedclothes. If it was summer time I would perch at the end of the bed, dangling my feet, and make up stories about the three characters portrayed there. My father replied, when questioned about the painting, that my grandparents had had it in their bedroom, and so from that time it took on an added meaning.

Set in an old-fashioned quite deep, black frame, the picture was of a small, poorly lit cottage kitchen, with a flagstoned floor, and a high, small, uncurtained window; the sill was empty except for a jar, and on the side above it there was a clock. A kindly old man was seated in a red winged chair, with arms outstretched to a small girl about to walk from her young mother's supporting hands to go to his embrace. A sleeping dog by the elderly person's feet completed the scene. The young mother was pretty and looked like mine, and the old man was, of course, to me my grandfather who had died soon after my birth. You can guess who the small child was supposed to be. During my lonely vigils, it truly fixed my imagination and I grew to love it very much.

My father often read snippets from letters his father had sent to him sometime before I was born, but especially from those received after I came on the scene. It was lovely to hear how Grandfather wrote about his newest grandchild, so lovingly and, though small as I must have been, as if already I was a person and belonged to the family. Those references and this special picture with the feelings it aroused in me, stirred up quite easily the sense of family ties and kinship, so needful for an only child. As I grew up and met some of my father's many brothers and his only sister, relationships slotted into place. Eventually, in my early teens, knowing then that my father was a lot older than my mother, he became for me that kindly grandfatherly figure in the armchair. I began to realise that he had so many qualities of an older person — calmness, patience, time for talking and the ability to listen. Now, when I look at it as an old lady myself, it reminds me also of the talents, skill, habits and mannerisms inherited from my parents, and their love and care of me and how much, in spite of everything that has happened over the years, I loved them, and still do, perhaps more so. My mother, knowing how I favoured that picture even as a child, gave it to me a few years before she died, and it now hangs above our bed in our retirement home.

Uncle Ernest, just two years older than my father, came to our shop very frequently, quite early in my life. He was in service in a big house nearby and was going to marry a friend of Mother's who was sleeping in our spare room at night and working each day with Uncle. Their marriage from our shop, some time after I was three, was my first conscious introduction to many of my father's family. Being so young then, there isn't much I can truly remember of that occasion except the feverish excitement on the wedding morning and odd little episodes during the day.

Auntie-to-be and my mother were both in my parents' bed that morning; I went to join them and had my very first delicious taste of grapes which the prospective bridegroom had left for his future bride. Never had I tasted anything so sweet and mouth-watering before, and I guess that my lasting and continued fondness for the fruit dated from that very morning.

Although it was most surely the very first remembered red-letter day of my life, I was too young to recall very much. The clothes worn as a very immature bridesmaid, and the bride's and older attendant's dress, didn't make any impression. There is one moment, though, etched quite clearly on my mind. Not being used to all that company in our house, and never having been to church before and not yet having discovered the joys of St Stephen's Church for myself, I was overcome with all the talk, singing and ceremony. Suddenly, feeling very alone standing at the altar with the older bridesmaid, a newly discovered twenty-year-old cousin, I yelled out pathetically, "I don't want to say my prayers; I want my Daddy." Bless him, he quietly came and took my hand and stood beside me until my duties were over. My mother must have felt sad, too, because she was overlooked. It was always my father I continually called for and not herself; at three, one has no tact or sensitivity, and as yet I didn't realise how hard was her life as mother and provider.

The wedding breakfast was good fun as three fresh cousins, more my own age, children of my father's younger brother Cecil, sat next to me and included me in their chat and later play. How I wished I had brothers and sisters like Pete, who was ten, Elsie seven, and Jean their little sister of five, and how I envied their fun and company with each other. From that brief meeting, throughout all my childhood and beyond, they were my hero and heroines. When the guests had departed and Auntie Agnes and Uncle Ern went away to live and work in Godalming, and no longer came to see us, how quiet it seemed. We didn't see these cousins again until I was over eighteen, apart from another blurred meeting at their home a little time later.

During the halcyon days before the Depression really took hold, and the threats of war were yet to come, there were one or two other red-letter days. Just before school started and after having measles, Father thought a day by the sea might do me good. Of course he couldn't leave the shop and join us, so Mother and her friend Mary, who lived nearby, organised a day out to the Londoner's haven — Southend. The train journey was much longer than the one to Liverpool Street, and gave me my very first glimpse and smell of the seaside.

Quickly I tucked my dress in my knickers, pulled off my shoes and socks, and danced up and down on the sand. The sea was very cold and took my breath away. There was such an expanse of water going on forever it seemed, so making sand pies suited me better. By the end of the day, just when we had to leave, I ventured up to my knees in the briny so that I could tell Dad about it. It had been a lovely day and we had our photographs taken by Auntie Mary — I still have the record . . . but it would have been perfect if someone else could have been there too.

Chicken-pox claimed me just before going up to the Juniors and kept me in quarantine most of the long summer holidays. So another treat was enjoyed by Mother and me at Dad's instigation. We paid a surprise, uninvited visit to Aunt Lily, his sister in Surrey. Our last meeting had been at the family wedding in the shop some five years before.

Mother had recently made nice matching dresses for both of us, which so impressed me; I remember they were mostly orange flowered ones. I also remember someone saying how nice we both looked as we boarded the Green Line bus. It was a beautiful country ride, once we had left London behind. We stopped at the Red House, Leatherhead, and started to walk after enquiring the direction to Auntie's house. We were stopped by being called from over the road by my cousin May, who had been a bridesmaid with me; she had spotted us leaving the bus stop as she and Auntie were about to ride home. There was great surprise and a pleasant welcome when they came over to us, and I remember clearly their remarks about how nice we looked in our new dresses. I was even more proud of my clever mother.

Having all missed the bus by then, and made to feel ten feet tall by their great pleasure, they walked us to their house chatting about May's recent engagement which at that moment wasn't very interesting to me, but was to prove so in the future. Auntie's house was much more modern and bigger than the rooms behind our shop. It was fairly new and had a proper bathroom, which certainly impressed both of us. I needed to go to the lavatory so many times, my mother thought I was unwell until the penny dropped!

The back of the semi-detached overlooked a lovely big field beyond, and Auntie's garden seemed enormous after our small patch. May was most kind to me and I really began to like both of them. The liking grew to real affection when they invited me to stay in the long summer break the next year. What joy there was in anticipating my first real holiday, and on my own too. In due course that promise was fulfilled on several occasions and opened the pleasures of country life to a city child.

Neighbours were kept at a distance. "People in business keep themselves to themselves," was my father's maxim, ". . . we don't want everyone to know our private affairs." My mother was much more friendly, and when she met folk out in the road or over the garden fence she always stopped for a chat.

The Hackshaws lived one side of the shop — Mrs Hackshaw did have a husband, but we never knew much about him, though I did think he had some really super suppers. At about six every night, his wife would break off if she was gossiping with Mum because she had to get Mr Hackshaw's evening meal. Their concrete yard was parallel with ours and their back door was opposite. In the warmer days, with all windows and doors open, delicious smells often flooded forth from their kitchen.

Their two children were quite a lot older than me, so we had little in common, but their big girl Eileen was the one who took me to school for a few months. She was quite kind to me when we were alone but feigned not to know me when her peers were around. Taking a neighbour's younger girl along must have cramped her style somewhat, and after that we had little contact. The Irish couple and their daughter, on the other side of our shop, have already been mentioned.

Most of the folk down Eden Road passed the time of day with us, but these people did not speak to us at all nor did they frequent the shop. With a very clever little girl about my age, they chose to send her to a more select church school at the top of our road and not the common council school I attended. We never played together, or even spoke in those days, but when we met up later at senior school she proved to be a very pleasant girl and was just as clever as her parents maintained. During the war we all moved away.

The main reason for the frequent quarrels between my parents and our Irish neighbours was our very untidy garden. They had primly planned theirs with a crazy paving path, a smooth, lush green lawn and colourful well-weeded flowerbeds. What I envied, though, was their lovely big apple tree. Besides bearing delicious fruit (they were always saying loudly how good the apples were), on hot summer days it cast a most welcome shade over Alma as she played with her toys oblivious of the covetous girl next door. Sadly, Father seemed too weak to garden, and also had to be ready to serve in the shop, and Mother was so overworked there certainly was no time for her to grow things or weed. I feel now, with hindsight, that our neighbours' constant complaints that the seeds from our weeds germinated among their cherished plants were true, and that our uncontrolled convolvulus, which travelled under the fence to strangle precious blooms, was also a reasonable complaint. It was a complete impasse and we never became even nodding acquaintances.

There were other folks we knew in the short street, mainly because of the shop. They and we could not have been very friendly as their names and faces now elude me. Having a shopkeeper for a father didn't seem to encourage friendships or even much neighbourliness for any of us, but of course that thought didn't occur to me at the time.

CHAPTER
FIVE

Enter Leonard

My brother, good morning: my sister, good night.
Hilaire Belloc

The only family Christmas remembered in any detail
was that of 1933. I was seven and a half years old (very
grown up now I was in the Junior School) and it
happened not long before the upheaval that changed all
our lives on that fateful April 21st, 1934. No family
festival, before or after, right up to the outbreak of the
Second World War can be recalled so clearly or so
happily as that Christmas. Pondering over the reason
why it should be so distinct so many years later, I came
to these alternative conclusions: perhaps it might be
because it was the last December which just involved
the three of us; or on the other hand, maybe, seven was
a most impressionable age and my memory was very
keen at that period; yet the dominant and nicest theory
seems to be that both my parents really wanted and
definitely planned to make it special, both for
themselves, but above all, special for their only child.
Knowing already how very different things might prove

to be from then on, and with improved finances, they both made a supreme effort. Anyway, I like to believe the latter case is the true one and it certainly was a lovely family occasion.

Every big and little happening seemed to lead up to the glorious climax of December 25th. That year even the pre-Christmas school activities were good and are etched on my mind. It was the first occasion I had been given the part of Mary in the class play that was to be acted in front of the whole school and then to visitors. My parents laughed, as I was to be the same character in St Stephen's celebrations. They remarked that they should have called me by my second name, which is also Mary, after Mother's friend, and how fervently I wished they had. The little play at school came from a book we shared, one between two, and we read the parts around the class as a sort of audition. The child sitting next to me then was either away or wasn't really interested because I recall being able to turn over the pages to prepare the next words Mary spoke well ahead of time, so desperately did I want that part in the final casting.

As already mentioned, progress in school work didn't interest Mother, but she loved anything connected with singing and drama and had herself produced little plays when a young girl, so she was keen to find blue and white material to make a traditional outfit for her daughter. We couldn't get the head-dress right, though — it kept slipping and once covered up the baby and caused Joseph to trip at the second performance. Yet, nothing daunted, the show continued and it was all very exciting and set the right atmosphere for the family celebrations.

It seems very strange now, looking back over these numerous years and bearing in mind how vivid all these incidents remained, that neither Mother nor I ever talked about this period, not even when we were a lot older and much closer again. Never mind, it is quite pleasing to recount the events now.

The shop certainly looked very smart and attractive. Father actually praised me and said what a good assistant I was becoming — no doubt maturity and ideas gleaned at school and Sunday School had improved my artistic capabilities. Business, as already mentioned, must have improved, if only temporarily; there were more fancy foods and packages on our premises, and we even bought more for our own consumption than we had in previous years. Tins and tins of biscuits, large ones — not the small, individually packed paper or cellophane packets we have these days — all of which were covered with pretty paper, narrowed our pathway round the back of the counter as Dad gradually served them in quantities of one or half pounds to our customers. Little triangular wafers with delicious brown fillings were my favourite, and chocolate-covered shortbreads that almost melted immediately in the mouth.

Some of his buddies gave me pennies, and one a whole silver sixpence in honour of the season. Several chocolate bars came my way, which hadn't this time to be paid for, luckily. I never recall such a feast of glorious goodies ever again in my childhood, or people being so generous during the next Christmas. The 1930s Depression must have overwhelmed us all after that as those awful years progressed.

How we all loved the activities involved in our domestic preparations; it was truly a family effort. How companionable it was to help as much as possible, and when we were together it didn't seem like work. We took our turn at mixing "the puds" under Mum's critical supervision. Our old scullery copper came into its own as the filled and covered basins boiled merrily inside. Dad acted as chief stoker whilst Mum was out doing her daily jobs. Never before had she made so many puddings, nor two rich fruit cakes. But they explained she was doing extra portions that year as, with little Joan now a toddler and Grandma and Uncle Tom rather frail, Uncle had thought that Aunt Ethel needed help and had asked Mother if she would mind doing extra quantities. As I've said before, Uncle Charlie was so thoughtful to his wife in many ways, and Mum always seemed to be able to fit in extra tasks in spite of her own workload, so she had cheerfully agreed.

Making jellies was my special task, and I wasn't above having a little taste of a jelly square as a just reward for my helpfulness. Dad did the blancmanges, and baking the mince pies late on Christmas Eve was Mum's last task. We three sat together after tea, just before my bedtime, with the chicken between us and a bath on the floor underneath the bird — it was time to pluck the feathers. That job was my least favourite of the preparations for the great day. It took so long, the feathers tickled my nose and made me sneeze and flew all over the scullery, however careful we tried to be; moreover, they were most difficult to gather up afterwards. Thinking about the poor chicken wasn't a good idea either, but it would be scrumptious to eat the next day, so the chore was continued to the bitter end, with high hopes for the morrow.

The night before Christmas is the one night in all the year when parents can be sure that their small fry will go early, and most willingly, to bed. It certainly proved to be the case with me. Hurriedly, when the poor bird was bare and naked, I dashed with relief into the darkness to the little room outside without one real qualm, then quickly returned, splashed my face with cold water and soaped my hands, unsuccessfully dried them, and raced up the stairs.

Our most recent lodger had left our abode. My parents explained that no more paying guests would be coming so the spare room was at last really mine. Mother lit my little candle, saying that she would soon return to settle me. As she left I frantically rummaged in the recesses of my special private drawer and eventually took out two hankies. The large one had the word "Daddy" embroidered in blue on the corner, and the smaller one had a pink stitched "Mummy", plus a little daisy-like flower. By the subdued flickering light, they were scrutinised critically. Yes! They still looked nice and quite clean considering I'd stitched them myself — my parents would be so pleased. Each one was carefully placed into a clean paper bag, begged secretly from Mum when I'd brought the shopping home from her interesting haberdashery store in the Baker's Arms.

Sewing wasn't my favourite pastime, but whilst she had been out working I'd done her hanky, letting Dad into that secret. I managed, by candlelight, to do his gift quickly in my bedroom, hiding it when feet were heard mounting the squeaky stairs — electric light wasn't used in the bedrooms now the lodgers were gone as this saved money. Carefully the little packages were safely hidden underneath the spare feather pillow. No-one would look there tonight, when goodnight kisses were given . . . they were far too busy. It had been no problem at all to go to bed early, but their last words as they left a snuggled daughter were "Now, dear, don't wake up before it is light tomorrow morning or we'll all be overtired on Christmas Day," and that was quite another matter. Obedience to that request I knew would be impossible and so, I fear, did they.

Suddenly, sitting up many hours later, with consciousness returning very quickly on that dark morning, I realised with real happiness that it must be Christmas Day at last. Had he been yet? I crawled hastily to the bottom of the bed, and with anxious hopeful fingers poked and prodded inside the big white pillowcase. Mum had put it up for me, casually remarking that I might need that instead of a stocking, so my aspirations had risen considerably . . . the complete answer to my letter might really happen after all. There was the usual round orange, some nuts, which I loved, fallen out of their little bag, something which could be a big waxy smooth apple and several little bundles which smelt like chocolate. Father Christmas must know that all my sweets from the shop had to be paid for out of my money-box. That was remarkably empty now, after paying for the hankies, as well as one for little Joan plus blue and pink silks for the sewing. Was there nothing else in my pillowcase? My heart seemed to miss a beat, and even now the deep resulting feeling of utter disappointment is easily recalled.

That short letter to Santa Claus had been done in my very best handwriting. Father had checked it and praised me for my neat and tidy written words. Mother had told me just where to put it up the now unused kitchen chimney. Where had we gone wrong? Could it be that now we didn't have a coal fire, he thought no-one lived in our shop? Was that why the longed-for pram and lovely doll hadn't been delivered? Not even the little afterthought, the pencil case, was there.

Back into the pillowcase went the inquisitive hands and there, standing on end, right in the corner, was something hard and sort of wooden, and it rattled. The lid pulled back, the top layer moved sideways and it seemed to have lots of things that felt like pens and pencils inside. Excitement increased. In the other corner, missed in the first investigation was a book, but this time there was no mistake about it, there were no other bigger toys. That's what comes from being too greedy, Elizabeth, I told myself! Miss Hayward, our new Sunday School teacher, had advised and warned us not to ask for too many things — it wouldn't be fair to all the other children. My faith in Father Christmas and his fairness to all children was much undermined by her remarks, but now it was being proved correct.

A call came from my parents' room. My none-too-quiet searching had disturbed them. "Has he been?" they kindly enquired. With tears of unhappiness welling up in my eyes, and leaping off the bed in my rush to tell them of my disappointment, I fell over something big and bulky at the foot of my sleeping place. Recovery was swift. Joyfully I shouted, "Mummy, Daddy, he has been and some presents are even too big for the pillowcase you gave me." My quickly drying eyes were seeing much better now with the light shining from the candle in their room. Yes, there was a lovely large dolly, beautifully dressed in clothes that seemed to be able to be taken off, and she was sitting in a pushchair! Oh dear! There was no proper pram! Quickly I came to Father Christmas's defence. Obviously he thought a seven-year-old with a sitting-up doll far too big for a baby carriage. Soon everything was on my parents' bed — the pillowcase, all its contents, the doll, the pushchair and, of course, their happy, wide-awake daughter. No more sleep for anyone. It was barely six o'clock. I'd never been up so early, and sadly their rest was already over too.

Much later that very special day Mother and I pushed my new gifts out for their first airing. The girl doll had lovely knitted vest, knickers, socks, dress, coat and hat, and even a pair of fancy, black-knitted shoes that laced together. Eventually, when Father Christmas was no longer believed in, I guessed who made those beautiful clothes. We had a circular walk round the houses to try out the real little pushchair and, hopefully, in my case, to meet someone we knew who would be impressed by the special presents.

It went very smoothly at first and "Joan" stayed sitting up very nicely, steadied by the proper straps. Then as we came to bumpy paving stones the wheels made a rattling noise, and sadly the wonderful gift lost its hundred per cent appeal. Of course I loved it and told my parents how pleased I was, yet it bothered me that although I wanted people to see it, I hadn't intended that they should hear it also. This was a very good lesson about learning to accept things for what they were, disappointments and all; nothing is absolutely perfect. From that day it wasn't wheeled about the streets very much, but I really enjoyed playing with it in the garden where on the rough bumpy earthy path and over the grass the noise was muted and it didn't make such a clattering sound.

The Sunday School Christmas party in the New Year really excelled itself, and for one adherent it was excellent. As usual there was the delicious tea, but the games period after that was very much shortened, and then we were all mysteriously seated to watch a very new amazing treat. A most generous person had donated money for the loan of a really early film projector and the hire of a very funny slapstick comedy film. The new box of tricks showed something which certainly must have appealed to the audience. I remember how we laughed, clapped and shouted our appreciation (the latter, something never done before), but nothing about the actual content of the novel presentation remains. With hindsight it must have been very jerky, but to all of us it was our initiation to silent films, and the flickering pictures and whirring sound held all the magic of the miraculous. That celebration brought a wonderful Christmas to a glorious end.

At about this time there were still one or two special items that could be bought on Sundays, quite against St Stephen's principles I fear. Street callers continued to ply their trade and seemed to have great delight in disturbing the grown-ups' afternoon nap, and certainly had the backing of their often bored brood of children once Sunday School was over. The loud ringing of the muffin man's bell advertised his presence. Cleverly balancing his tray on his head, he would walk down Eden Road hoping for some response from the closed doors and unnaturally silent street. Some families did sample his wares but there is no memory of our household doing so. He couldn't have been as popular as the other Sunday traders because he soon stopped coming.

Another travelling salesman wheeling his small stall around the road and shouting out his wares was the fishmonger, carrying cockles, mussels and shrimps. My mother loved these delicacies. Being a real cockney, until her marriage she had often indulged her passion in the Bermondsey market, and at Southend on her many youthful trips to the Londoners' seaside mecca. Now and again, no doubt when the week's business had been reasonably brisk, she managed to inveigle Father into letting us have half a pint of shrimps for our Sunday tea and, very occasionally, a few mussels and cockles for herself. Neither he nor I liked those other fishy tit-bits.

During the summer months Wall's ice-cream tricyles would chirpily tinkle their bells, and at these times children poured out of their usually quiet Sunday homes with halfpennies clutched tightly in hot sticky hands to "Stop me and buy one!" The Snowfrutes were sheer nectar to childish taste-buds, and during really hot spells I was permitted to dip into my resources and for a brief spell was in a seventh heaven. All my former concerns about keeping the Sabbath Day holy were conveniently forgotten.

Being in the Junior department at school brought new responsibilities. There must have been a concerted effort by the staff to encourage their pupils to be smarter and cleaner. Our teachers told us that we were all big enough now to shine our own shoes and mustn't expect our parents to do this chore for us any longer. Also our nails ought to be brushed regularly and not bitten. There were sudden and unannounced inspections after prayers some mornings; it was amazing how these check-ups never seemed to happen when I had eventually managed a really special effort. It was most provident for the girls that in muckier times of the year we were usually wearing our much-hated black itchy woollen stockings — they just got a bit dustier after frantically rubbing shoes up and down the backs of our legs as each class was lined up. White ankle socks in the better weather meant only our bare legs suffered, which could quickly be wiped over in the lavatories afterwards.

Local carnivals were a very popular summer attraction in many London areas. Walthamstow had an annual one, which I recall supported the local hospital. Mother, with her usual flair and great enthusiasm, went to town on one well-remembered occasion. Shredded Wheat had very recently become a special breakfast treat for us, and she decided to enter me in the seven-and-under children's fancy dress section as a portion of that favourite cereal. From the nether regions of our shop Dad produced some darkish yellow crepe paper, which she crinkled up and made a sort of dress for me. She cut strips from the bottom up to the waist and added other such layers to the skirt so it looked like a Shredded Wheat. One cut-up Shredded Wheat box made a crown, and fronts and backs of other boxes were stitched onto the bodice and back of the paper dress, clearly displaying the name of the product. To complete the outfit I carried a packet in Mum's basket, tied up with spare yellow crepe paper. How proud I felt as I walked along carrying a money-box I'd been given to collect pennies from the crowds lining the route, and prouder still of the badge proclaiming 1st prize in the seven-and-under class. Yet I cannot remember, for the life of me, what reward I actually received.

Up to this time, while Mum still did some cooking for us, there were several occasions when I helped her to make pastry. At first, when I was under five, she just gave me some of her mixture. My! How swiftly that lump changed from a white ball to a mucky mess once my hands had kneaded it and rolled it out. The yucky

73

soft gooey consistency that stuck relentlessly to my fingers really nauseated me. Even the birds weren't too keen to eat the greyish biscuits — certainly not us. Later, Mother encouraged me to rub in fat and shape and cook some jam tarts produced entirely by her daughter's own, not so fair, hands. My very obliging father nobly and gingerly ate one of the offerings this time, yet the apprentice wasn't that comfortable about sampling her own wares. Sadly, later still, when recipes could have been carefully followed and proper food could have been prepared and cooked by a slightly older child, there was no time or money to ensure the project.

Mother and her friend helped me to knit, so that I could do this fairly successfully at school, but sewing never came easily. Being left-handed complicated the learning, and Mum hadn't much spare time to teach her slow and difficult offspring. Crochet work was never mastered, although Mum did try to teach me on one occasion.

I have a rather vague recollection of seeing Uncle Cecil, his wife, also an Aunt Lily, and my three cousins Peter, Elsie and Jean, in a very lovely place somewhere in Crookham, Hampshire. Mother and I just had a day visiting them and I know we played hide-and-seek in their large garden, and leaving them was a rather sad affair. Apart from this game, there is little I can recall, but my appetite to see and hear more of these exciting relatives was well and truly whetted. However, no more meetings materialised until during the war, although

Uncle Cecil came to see us at the shop before the war began.

Around this time my father's gambling exploits began to register with me. He had succumbed to Littlewoods football pools. The hope was that his system of selection would give his syndicate of friends and cronies a wonderful hoped-for windfall; that would then solve all our money problems. Perhaps he would even be able to sell 80 Eden Road and buy a new business in his beloved county of Surrey. It might even be near Godalming, the little country town of his birth.

Loving school as I did, the disused football coupons with all the teams listed like children's names, and the little squares alongside to mark with 1, 2 and 3, were like a teacher's proper register, and made my solo game of schools much more realistic. Matched to perfection, as Dad began to indulge in football pools, Miss Hayward began to do what Miss Tintsel had started a few years before, except this time it was not the keeping the Sabbath Day holy commandment; this new teacher started to wage war on the evils of gambling.

Again, my very quiet and unsuccessful father was implicated, and perhaps my mother, but as before he was much more involved — she only posted the coupon. Once more their very concerned child was torn in two. It would be so wonderful for my mother, for all of us, to have a nice big shop in the country. Since visiting Aunt Lily in Leatherhead, that had become my ideal place in which to live. Unfortunately we could only achieve this wish through the pools, and that was gambling and wrong. Unfortunately, also the checking of his score usually had to be done on Sunday morning when the Sunday paper (another sin) arrived with the listed results. Adding salt to the wound and really implicating their daughter, both parents asked me to pray for a win each night and when I went to the Sunday service. Life was certainly becoming very complicated, nothing was clear-cut and everything we did seemed to be breaking God's laws. Guilt hovered over me, especially every time I quietly continued to go to St Stephen's.

As spring burst forth in 1934, my usually energetic and very busy mother appeared to be constantly weary and she had a number of days away from her cleaning jobs. I hoped she wouldn't be too ill. It couldn't really be explained but I began to think she looked fatter and certainly didn't dash about as much as she had. There weren't so many cuddles, and jumping into bed with her on Sunday mornings wasn't encouraged either. She and Father often abruptly stopped talking when I came into the room and the phrase "Little piggies have big ears" was frequently quoted and that really puzzled me. We lived in a town and there were no pigs in our road. Visits to see cousin Joan had stopped, and several unmentioned and unopened bulky parcels were being stored in my bedroom cupboard. Dad seemed quite worried and very very quiet, and often had headaches when I came home from school. He didn't play with me, talk to me or help me so much with my homework. Something intangible, yet noticeable, seemed very wrong. I hoped that both my parents weren't very ill and that they wouldn't die. Since Blackie had been unwell and died, illness had become connected with certain death in my mind.

Then one amazing day all became perfectly clear. Mother rather mysteriously said that she had something most important to tell me. What she said made me sit up quickly with both ears truly listening and both eyes nearly popping out of my head. Was it really true what I had just heard? Was my longed-for wish and constant request to both parents at last going to be fulfilled? Yes, Mother had just said we were going to have a baby quite soon in our family. My interpretation of her wonderful news was this; there was going to be a little sister to play with and care for. This was even better, much better than birthdays or Christmas — far more exciting.

Mother went on to explain that she was going into hospital to get the most precious commodity and that she hoped I'd be a good girl for Daddy and help him whilst she was away. As if she had to say such a thing — of course I'd be good, especially as my most constant prayers were being answered. Then I heard both parents talking together a few days later about a lovely new maternity or baby hospital that was due to be opened in Walthamstow and the very first one to be born there would receive special presents. They hoped our new baby would win the prizes. Everything was so exciting, I just couldn't wait.

I began to think what a big sister ought to do to get ready for the newcomer. First of all my halfpennies and occasional pennies must be saved up; no more sweets would be bought from the shop; then when I'd, hopefully, got a full money-box, she could have a very special present from me. How the plans grew. Every waking moment, and some of my dreams, seemed to be spent thinking and deciding what we could do together. Although I knew that babies were little and fairly helpless (my cousin Joan proved this), somehow in my vivid imagination our family addition would be different, and she would arrive dressed exactly like me and would be able to walk and talk and play and even share my double bed. What a good thing that the spare room was now mine and was big enough to take two children.

The excitement grew. Soon all those unwrapped parcels were opened. The nappies and new white towels were washed and stored away. The little clothes Mum had been making and I had hoped were for my doll were clearly knitted for my little sister. The final evidence of the pending arrival was that my lately vacated small bed in my parent's bedroom was dismantled, and put in the very tiny box room off mine, and the stored cot was brought from the back of the cupboard and put next to my mother's side of their bed. It couldn't be long to wait now.

Whilst helping my parents to get out the old cot from the cupboard in my bedroom ready for the new baby, a strange discovery was made. On the high shelf, which I hadn't been able to reach until then, were several pictures rather like big texts of Jesus with a large red heart, and the writing underneath mentioned his sacred heart. Also there was reference to "Our Lady", and the pictures of her made me realise that she and Mary, the mother of Jesus, were the same person. Beside a very long string of funny black beads with a cross, was an eight-inch-wide framed picture with what looked like proper straw inside the glass, on which a doll-like halo-ed baby was lying with a big red heart. Surely that was a manger scene? When I asked what these things were and why they were hidden away, Mother quickly brushed my enquiries aside, except to say they were hers and that Dad didn't want us to talk about them. This was the first indication I had that my mother's religion wasn't quite the same as my father's — yet neither of them seemed to go to church, not even to St Stephen's.

Like my poor parents' high hopes and aspirations, the one wish that their second child would be the first arrival born in the new hospital was sadly dashed. The new family member was born two weeks early, and when I got up on 21st of April Mum wasn't there. Dad said she'd gone already to fetch the baby and that I now had a little brother. A little brother! How that information stunned and staggered me. Not only did the penny drop at last with the sudden appearance of a second-hand pram in our living room, and Dad's description of the new arrival that it really was a tiny baby like all the others, but it was also a boy! What a double disappointment was mine.

We had a baby boy in our family! I had a brother! That outcome had never entered my head for one moment. I had wanted a sister or nothing. Disappointment took over, and sadly I cried not a little. After a comforting chat and the promise of a visit to see

Mother and the little one after school, Dad convinced me a bit that all would be well and that I'd quite like the newcomer. I skipped off to school quite pleased, although a slight niggle still remained that somehow we'd all been cheated, but the thought of the sensational news to tell my teacher and classmates cheered me up no end.

Everyone seemed to be round Miss Macdonald's desk that morning and all had things to tell her — nothing so marvellous as my news of course — but a lot of patience was required as I waited. Then the moment for disclosure arrived. "Miss Macdonald, our baby's come and it's a boy." I almost deafened her. Her quick and sharp reply absolutely deflated her bubbly pupil. "Don't shout, Elizabeth! What a pity he won't be able to come to this Junior Girls' School." The recent newly acquired cheerfulness disappeared, the sun left the sky and the rains came again. Quickly and tearfully, I crept to my desk. Fortunately that rejection was softened. Some of my classmates were duly impressed at playtime. By the end of lessons, excitement had returned once more at the thought of the evening visit.

It was a proud moment to be out with my father, and good to know that I would see Mother again . . . and my brother. She hadn't been away for more than one night and day and yet, as we entered the ward, shyness overcame me and at first I hung back. Peeping round the door, she was smiling and opened her arms for me. Letting go of my father's hand, I ran to greet her. With a pretty bed jacket round her shoulders, Mother looked much better now and hugged and kissed me, and then together we looked at our baby boy. How tiny he was and so wrinkled, much smaller than cousin Joan had been (I'd forgotten she had been over a month old when we first saw her). I had a good peep at him. His little nails were so small and pink and he made funny little snuffly noises. Measuring my big hands against his, I put my thumb into his little palm. Suddenly he gripped my thumb with his tiny fingers. As it did when Blackie first snuggled up against me, love for this brother of mine — though he wasn't the longed-for sister — just flooded through me.

What did Miss Macdonald know about dear little babies — he was ours, he was mine, and of course he would have to go to the Boys' Junior School, but that didn't matter at all. Mother told me that he was to be called Leonard Ernest. These were Uncle Cecil's second name and Uncle Ern's first. Unfortunately my parents called him Lennie for quite a while, but to me he was always Leonard or Len. I was no longer an only child. Now there was another member in our family . . . my little baby brother.

CHAPTER
SIX

A Miscellany of Memories

Where to the sessions of sweet thought
I summon up remembrances of things past.

Although the shop and my home with its vicinity and local interests are mentioned at the start of this narrative, the first, happiest and most constant recurring memories are not of these or any other happening, nor yet of any particular member of our extended family. Strangely enough, they weren't even connected with my beloved father who was the dominant adult in my early life, and to whom I was closer than to any other human being for many years. No, it was not any special red-letter day or remarkable moment, nor was it about an affectionately attached unrelated person. These most precious early recollections were and still are of my lovely enchanting mother, who later featured so little as a loving parent during my childhood.

In my mind's eye, there is a very clear vision of a smiling, often laughing, very carefree person. Always singing and always cuddling me, she demonstrated physically how much she loved her little daughter during those few blessed years. This picture did begin to blur, however, as dire poverty reared its ugly head, and even more so when she herself was at last free from drudgery and oppressive work. Somehow even then the cheerful optimistic loving nature was only just there under the surface until distance and time lessened our bonds, yet it soon returned when she was a grandma and a very old lady.

These most pleasing early memories were never really forgotten and have been so easy to recall. Now in old age myself, they are remembered with enjoyment and great poignancy. In spite of having to char at the beginning of her marriage, when at that time women usually did not seek employment, and to take in washing right from the beginning of motherhood, my parents were not so poor in those days and there were some spare moments to be together and we really did enjoy them.

To her small offspring she was very pretty, her brown eyes sparkled, and her long dark hair waved back into a neat roll. She was always so perky and, with her melodious voice, a very joyful personality. I know I was cared for tenderly and delightfully played with.

With hindsight, that marvellous belated explanation of difficulties and problems, I now realise that my mother had basically an optimistic, outgoing, happy-go-lucky nature. More than anything else, she earnestly desired to please everyone with whom she had dealings, a truly impossible task, and one increasingly less possible as her economic position deteriorated. Sadly, hard times gradually and ruthlessly pulled her down and deadened her buoyant spirit. Yet for a brief period her natural disposition showed through, and I was on the receiving end of this happy state. It truly coloured my earliest memories of her.

Together we would laugh and giggle as we worked and played in the room behind the shop or when we went on outings. She'd push me on swings and roundabouts, dress me up in her clothes and in those she'd made for me. Above all, mundane tasks like shopping, housework and cooking were great fun with her. Singing would break out at any moment. *This little piggy went to market* and *Round and round the garden like a teddy bear* were my earliest pop songs interspersed with more active ones like *Ring a ring of roses* and *Oranges and lemons*. Nursery rhymes were continually on our lips. She often hugged and kissed me, something my father never did until I left home to visit or go to school, and then it was only a parting peck. At bedtime, lullabies were soothingly crooned to her little daughter: "Go to sleep my baby, close your pretty eyes" or "Do you want the moon to play with, or the stars to run away with, they'll come if you don't cry" were the most popular ditties, although probably misquoted with the passage of time. Yet their comforting words and melodies spelt security and love to the baby they rocked to sleep.

Most mornings Mother went charring in one or two of the larger houses bordering on the edge of Epping Forest. It was then that my father acted as nursemaid.

Sometimes, though, Mum was able to take me with her; the rest of the day she would be at home. A little later our affairs must have deteriorated somewhat because to increase the family budget she had to take in washing and ironing for folk. Then there was the occasional lodger occupying our spare bedroom. The shop was obviously not attracting enough custom and Father didn't try any other employment himself, he never did. These additional chores were even more demanding of my female parent's time and energies. From then on she had less to do with me and Dad took over most of my care; although she was in the house and I did see her, she had many other more pressing jobs than to deal with her daughter.

Mum hated being so busy. On several occasions I remember asking her not to go out cleaning nor to keep washing so much; then she sat me on her lap and promised that one day she would just be an ordinary housewife and my mummy. Now I realise that was always her heartfelt wish but sadly it never materialised until late into what should have been her retirement years. Then she was well over 70. My poor mother had a dreadfully hard married life. Her husband certainly had a less arduous time and, gradually, with little to do in the shop, he took over her role in the house and the parenting.

The first recollection occurred very early in childhood, yet it was truly remembered by me and not because it was frequently talked about. Neither of my parents ever mentioned it until suddenly, much later, when "messy" described our living quarters and I recalled that incident. Mother immediately agreed that it had taken place and was amazed at my memory of something so far back. I was sitting in my pram, and that was sold when I was about two and a half, indicating roughly my age. A little furry thing began to tickle my feet. It fascinated me, but Mother, noting my interest and seeing what it was, shouted for Dad and he acted swiftly. Yes, it was a mouse, and my outgoing mother told me later that she had always been terrified of them. In those early days, she continued, there was an occasional mouse in the shop, but that was the only one to make an appearance in our living quarters. What would health inspectors say about that fact today? Anyway, Dad was nearby and quickly disposed of it. Fortunately both parents laughed and I joined in as well. Perhaps that is why mice have never scared me. If only there had been such an early reassuring encounter with spiders!

Although a less dramatic and demanding parent, Dad spent hours talking to me, and through that I sensed his love and care. He was always ready to tell stories, but he mostly read to me, pointing out pictures and matching words, which encouraged my desire to read and learn. At that time, before ill health troubled him, he was so calm and patient and so different from Mother; they certainly complemented each other. He was a quiet yet entertaining companion, friend and teacher — my mother was a happy, optimistic and outgoing parent. How blessed I was to have two such contrasting yet loving people around.

Where folk lived, the type of house they had, how many occupied the same building, whether it was a private or business establishment and, above all, the kind of front door they possessed, always intrigued me especially when very young. This avid curiosity was no doubt fostered by being an only child, and rather a lonely one at times. There were occasions when both parents were very busy; then it was interesting to sit by their bedroom window, where I also slept, and watch the world go by.

The children in our street who had brothers and sisters were greatly envied, especially as I saw them go into their homes and firmly shut the door behind them. Ours was always open, it had to be, certainly at that time during my waking hours, and customers never had to knock but just walked in: the tinkling bell warning us of their arrival. Even more important and disturbing was the fact that as a result of this constant observation other children seemed to go out far more often and not with just one parent only but with both; moreover, they seemed to have more visitors than we did.

This rather unnatural interest in our neighbours became a great obsession, particularly whilst I was an only child. It was quite absorbing to live secondhand watching their comings and goings, imagining what they were about to do and where they were going. So little seemed to happen in our home. How I longed for us three to be more like them! Why couldn't Dad come with Mum and me to see our relations like other fathers seemed to do? Why couldn't we go for a walk all together? Why didn't Dad go out to work and Mum stay at home? The shop always seemed to be the reason why we could not do normal things and my hatred of it increased.

When both my parents were occupied, their bedroom became not only a look-out tower but also a rest room, and a playroom, especially when the days were inclement and the garden and shop were out of bounds. As a change from spying on the neighbours, my parents' wardrobe would become my secret home. It had a door to open and close. Their clothes and shoes would be pushed to the far end to give some space to turn into a room with the aid of cushions, pillows and boxes for the furniture, plus dolls for companions, so that I could enact my solitary game of "Mothers and Fathers". Eventually, when school days started and mental stimulation came from fairy tales, this closet changed from home to castle prison to a dungeon, even into a witch's cave, as did the shop at times. The lighter, less cluttered bedroom was much less frightening than our business premises and so much more preferred for imaginative games.

Wistfully wearying of solitary play, I'd see my peers enjoying the current children's games in Eden Road after school during the lighter evenings and in the holidays. How I longed to join them. However, in their more affluent days, both parents were united in the conviction that their cherished little one must never be allowed in the street with the "riff raff". Yet how I longed to join in their fun, especially as not one of these interesting boys or girls was ever allowed beyond our counter and certainly not in our garden to play with me.

Whilst snugly in the cot beside my parents' bed, just before school began, something in their room began to trouble me. With the changing of the seasons and putting the hour forward or back, sleeping patterns also changed and I began to waken very early in the lighter mornings. Lying very quiet, listening to my parents' steady breathing, wishing they would open their eyes too, I began to notice a queer-looking old man with a pointed hat appearing by the wall behind the clock on the mantle shelf. Dreading to open my eyes, I peered between my slightly opened fingers hoping and hoping he'd not be there. My parents never seemed to waken and I longed for them to do so, yet I was too frightened to call them.

The fireplace over which the spectre always manifested itself had never had a fire burning in its grate since the morning of my birth. Father had told me many times that it had been so cold then, although it was June, that he had lit it for Mother and me. This frequently requested and earnestly devoured tale made me feel so special and very, very wanted. Since then there had never been a fire in that grate and that fact seemed to prove all the more how much he loved us. It was good to remember it often, especially if Dad was cross with Mum, and rather quiet with me. Now, with the sudden appearance of this horrible apparition, that lovely story was being spoiled. Each time I furtively glanced that way this little old man looked as though he would pounce on me, his terrified victim.

Gradually I began to discover he could be quite small, yet at other times he got bigger and bigger. Often he was almost invisible and, happily, sometimes never there at all. Mostly though, he was clearly defined. Reason and understanding slowly dawned. He came and went with the brightness or dullness of the early morning light. Fortunately Dad and I had recently been talking about sunshine and shadows and how the position of the sun affected the size of the shadow; moreover, how they completely disappeared on dull days. Yet when this solution came, and in spite of his chatting on this very subject, I just couldn't tell him or Mother of my fears and worries. Reticence was second nature to me as a child, but I did sort that problem out by myself in the end, when I noticed the similarity of the shape of the clock to the pixie-like man with his pointed hat. Then, contrariwise, I looked forward to seeing the little old man and was disappointed when he didn't put in an appearance. So the nightmare concerning wizards and ghosts had a happy ending.

As many children have nightmares, so did I from time to time. Between the ages of four and seven any unguarded talk about bonfires, smoke or flames, any sign of dirty black fumes coming from our hated oil stove, or any sudden noises that whooshed or roared just before bedtime, would make me reluctant to leave my parents. This particular fear became very prevalent just after our living room chimney caught fire. From then on the merest whiff of burning garden refuse, soot or smoke, even our neighbours' burnt toast wafting over the fence, would conjure up scary memories of

90

that awful time. Yet my parents never knew from me why on occasions their usually co-operative daughter became reluctant to go to bed.

However, the most common bad dreams that so tortured my early childhood were of unrecognisable enormous machinery, and of being lost among the loathsome things. These visions had no definite shape for ages but were of very huge greasy and black objects consisting of cogs going round and round, or larger oily iron shafts working up and down and backwards and forwards, noisily and relentlessly disturbing peaceful slumbers. Hissing, spiteful steam would spit and splutter out of these monstrosities, everywhere would be sombre grey and it all troubled me greatly.

As with other anxieties, these nightmares caused much thought and, slowly but surely, there seemed to be a reasonable explanation. Our trips to Deptford to see Grandmother and Auntie Ethel always necessitated Mother and me going to Liverpool Street Station where we saw at very close quarters gigantic engines and vast rolling stock, so enormous and dwarfing to a small child. The short cut to the road outside, where we always caught the bus, took us through the sooty, smoky, screeching backways to the station. Eventually it became logical to me that the monsters in the bad dreams were the snorting giants echoing through the dirty, sooty terminus.

Going to school increased my knowledge and confidence, and suddenly it was exciting to hear the clamour and shattering noise and smell the musty steam and smoke. These nightmares disappeared soon after Senior School began. Other pressures and stresses coloured waking and sleeping hours then. Yet, as before, when I remember the cause for calling out and needing my parents, I also recollect that I never told them the reason for the distress. So again, needless heartache and suffering was endured. Perhaps even in those early days my parents' greater distresses were already being assimilated by their offspring and made me loath to give them more worries.

Yet it wasn't all doom and gloom, or all nightmares; visions of hope and beautiful dreams also cheered my life. When we did have visitors or red-letter days, happy dreamy slumbers were remembered in the morning. Most of these more cheerful imaginings, however, were variations on a familiar theme, namely the three of us living in a smart private house with its own, usually red, front door tightly closed. Of course there was no concrete approach to the dwelling, just attractive gardens full of colourful flowers. In other dreams we'd all go for walks in a spacious park with at first a doll's pram like the one in my favourite book. As the desire matured, the baby doll in the carriage became a little hoped-for sister dressed just like me. The best aspect of all these dreams was that both parents were present and together.

Mother loved to entertain in those early days and was in her element on the few occasions when relations or friends came to see us. Unfortunately, even then when finances were a little healthier, I realise now my parents were never rich enough to enable her to give full rein to her ideas of being a good hostess. She was basically very flamboyant and dramatic. Father, on the other hand, was often a wet blanket about having guests. Most of these proposed ventures would start an argument between my parents. Why did she want to have folk anyway and why invite so many — yet usually it was only one or two, and what about the cost?

If Mother won the battle, and she did sometimes, then that began another set of queries. What did she propose to give them to eat? "It will only need to be a few bits and pieces; they wouldn't expect much," Dad would always counter. He was cautious where expense was involved. Mum was the exact opposite and loved to be generous, often to the extent of foolishness. She really knew how hard she had to work and the state of their financial situation, yet eventually he must have gone along with her plans most times, because before schooldays claimed their daughter, and for just a short while afterwards, there were three lots of visitors who came fairly regularly — Uncle Ern and Aunt Agnes very frequently before their marriage, Mother's friend Mary, and, of course, Auntie Ethel and Uncle Charlie.

Catering for these people usually meant first of all a trip to the Baker's Arms shopping centre, or even the High Street on Saturday evenings if the visit happened on Sunday. Flour and extra bread was always top of the list of requirements, but the main item, after those two articles, was eggs. As far as can be recalled, there were only egg or sardine sandwiches for these teas, with a decoration and added filling of mustard and cress if the money stretched that far. It was for her own baking, though, that most of the eggs were needed, and with them, plus the flour, Mum really went to town.

How enjoyable were the morning's preparations! There was always some sort of fruitcake to cook — "Men enjoy that," was her regular comment. My own particular favourites were her little Bakewell tarts, small, crispy Madeira cakes, and a lovely chocolate sponge, covered on really important occasions with chocolate icing. Scraping out the yellow mixing bowl was the expected highlight of those proceedings and helped assuage my mouth-watering hunger. As her daughter fetched and carried and tried to beat up the eggs, there were little titbits along the way too. Mother always maintained that the cook should know what her efforts tasted like before giving them to her visitors, and that suited her helpmate. Cooking was no hardship for Mother, if she could afford to do it properly and with some finesse. She was a very sociable person.

With the delicacies all prepared, we would busy ourselves clearing up. The singing would increase now that the real concentration was over. We would flit about dusting and tidying. Next we would wash and change, putting on matching pinnies ready for the final spurt. Out of the fireside cupboard would come one of her prettily embroidered tablecloths and a matching traycloth, both trimmed with her own crocheted edging, probably all stitched for her bottom drawer a few years before. The best china would be washed and I would carefully put it out with the knives and spoons, counting the places as I did so.

As we progressed, my excitement grew and grew. Mum would be very chirpy too, but Father just got gloomier and gloomier. At last, when all was ready and the kettle was whistling, the shop doorbell would tinkle cheerfully and in would come the expected company. Mother and I would be most welcoming, and once they were actually in our home, Dad's expression would lighten and he would be friendly and pleasant too. My anxious heart would lift wonderfully as his words softened in the convivial atmosphere. We had mostly happy tea parties in those early days. Mother would have been even more of a supportive wife if Father had been a conventional bread-winning husband.

Electrical storms created real havoc in our household. Even a suspicion of a flash of lightning or the slightest, almost unrecognisable murmur of thunder produced terror and near hysteria in my mother. Any hot sultry day, with the above minute signals and a sudden darkening of the sky, would trigger off a predictable chain of events. Curtains would be hastily pulled, mirrors covered quickly with tea towels, and knives, scissors and any other shiny objects would be whisked out of sight. Then, unless there was a speedy lessening of the depression, worse was to come. Once a definite clap of thunder was heard or a genuine bright flash of lightning observed, mother, plus daughter, would soon be seated on the boxed-in stairway. In this hideaway, when all the solid doors top and bottom of the well were closed, no chink of light could disperse the darkness and there was never a bulb in the bayonet holder at the top of the stairs so it was always absolutely lightproof and, to a small child, more frightening than the actual storm. Father did not join us. Storms never bothered him, and of course there was the shop to look after. He would tell us when all was over.

That was the daytime procedure. Somehow it seemed even more disturbing and scary if the upset happened at night. Many a deep sleep was broken as I was rudely lifted out of my snug bed, wrapped in a blanket, and deposited once more on the hard dark stairs. Mother was never known to slumber through the quietest tempest. Again, Father never joined his family. He often remonstrated with her about waking me when I was soundly sleeping, but she compulsively had to seek refuge in a darkened, enclosed area, and always had to take her daughter with her. It's just amazing that I'm not more concerned about storms today.

A similar reaction was instigated when the historic R101 went over our shop just before it crashed in France. Mother hastily declared that I'd be frightened by the noise and the sight of such a dreadful machine. Much later she explained to me about the Zeppelin raids on London during the 1914–18 war and how terrified she'd been then. Perhaps that experience had triggered off her panic reaction to storms, etc. Dad took the other view about this famous means of travel, and thought I'd like to witness the flight of such a splendid airship. Anyway, this time he had his way and encouraged me to watch with him. I thought it quite strange but exciting, and the sad end later proved it to be all the more an historic event to have witnessed.

Poor Mother shut herself in her usual hiding place, alone this time.

Cinema-going became very popular as the 1930s progressed, but even at the beginning of the decade it was taboo for us, not because it was regarded as being wicked, and not only on account of its cost, though that did hold some sway. An additional prohibitive factor was that Dad didn't like any of us mixing with so many people in a close, dark, foggy atmosphere. In spite of this stated disapproval, someone, probably Mum's friend Auntie Mary, took us both to witness my first film show when I was about four or five. The only scene remembered was of a man having a bath, not in a tin one off the fence like ours, but in a proper modern bath in a modern bathroom with taps to turn on to fill it with water and a plug pushed in a hole to stop the water running away. Such luxury was then a wonderful mystery to me.

I watched the whole sequence avidly, bemused to see people, not really with us, walking about and talking so we could hear them — we couldn't talk or walk with them, yet we could even see them having a bath. Then the water was suddenly emptied. At that point the camera's focus left the man, and when it next returned to him the bath was empty and strangely the man was also gone. For many a day and night after that I was most puzzled and worried, wondering where the man had disappeared to. Had he gone down the hole with the water? Until I saw Aunt Lily's lovely modern bathroom a few years later and enjoyed a bath in it myself, really knowing how very small the hole was, the answer to that question had always concerned me. I left the cinema that day most relieved actually to know that our bath hung on a nail on the fence and didn't have a hole in it. My father, with Mum's help, filled and emptied it with hot water from the kitchen copper. So it was all right in our house — no-one could possibly disappear. Somehow I don't think my poor parents would have shared my relief and opinion if there had been a choice. Bath time for them, if only once a week, must have been very hard work.

From the very first glimmers of knowing right from wrong and approval from disapproval, Elizabeth Cronk couldn't bear to know that she had transgressed and made her parents cross. It was the end of my world to be at odds with anyone, and that included our extended family and Sunday and day school teachers. I was a very co-operative and obedient child who wanted to please, and I seldom had to be checked, but when it did happen I would resent correction strongly to begin with and would sometimes feel silent with rage, but only briefly. Then guilt, remorse and sorrow would overwhelm me, resulting in floods of tears. After that I would be desperate to put matters right and be in tune with those whom I had offended.

So distressed and upset I'd become that, however trivial the misdemeanour, it was difficult to recover my equilibrium and really deep-seated sobs would rack my body for several hours after all was forgiven and forgotten. The great need to please and to be accepted and to have a friendly family was fundamental to my make-up right from the very beginning. This feeling was much increased and intensified during the war when living in other people's homes. Knowing they were very kind to put up with me, and that I was in their debt, made me even keener to do the correct thing and fit in. This outlook and attitude of being willing to do almost anything to keep the peace with those I really loved has continued to a slightly lesser degree right up to the present day. Even now, at the age of seventy, any truly upsetting and unhappy disagreement will leave heavy sighs and sobs to shake my body long after reconciliation, which is not very adult behaviour but rather hard to change now.

"Percy! I nearly died and felt so ashamed of our very naughty little girl. She actually attacked Doctor Buchan," declared my affronted and shaken mother. Father had just come to my cot in their bedroom, after the doctor had left, to see how I had fared after his visit. Truly amazed and obviously disbelieving, he surveyed his daughter safely tucked up in bed, looking peaky, spotty and woebegone. "Oh no! Not our Elizabeth, she couldn't do that, she's a good girl!" However, my hangdog expression and silent response must have given proof to Mum's accusations, and my fond father looked very disappointed and sadly patted my head. Seeing my quivering lips and tears welling up in my eyes, Mother quickly relented, and putting her arms round me said, "She didn't really mean to; she just isn't well. It's measles as we thought, and she has to stay in bed for a while," then she smiled at me.

Yet I did mean it! I was really angry and outraged, though I hadn't wanted to make my parents sad. I'd never been properly ill before and had never seen any doctor until that day. He had cheerfully come into our room, said a quick "Hello" to both of us, adding, "Now let me have a look at these spots." Elizabeth Cronk was not used to such familiarity from strangers, especially when feeling poorly. Then he actually went on to lift my nightie. Weak though I was, I still remember that my reaction was swift. I threw my pillow at his head, aiming very accurately, and I ferociously pushed him away after that.

From a usually quiet biddable little girl, this was heavy aggressive resistance, and most unexpected and outrageous behaviour which shamed my poor mother. Thankfully our doctor only laughed at my actions and attitude and tried another approach, which was much more successful, and never again did I react in such an unruly way to Dr Buchan. Regular as clockwork, during the next three years, I was his patient, having contracted childish complaints like whooping cough, chicken-pox and overgrowing my strength and becoming anaemic during the long school summer holiday, but from then on I was quietly acquiescent to all physicians and medical people.

Apart from these usual illnesses, I was and have been a very fit person. Even when we became too poor to afford regular and healthy food, my energy and natural robustness never deserted me. There was one little problem that constantly beset me in those early childhood days however, and it always happened at the weekend, particularly on Sunday.

Sunday was then the highlight of our week for several reasons. Both parents were more relaxed on that day. Mother didn't go out to work and seldom had washing to do for other folk, unless the weather had been very unfavourable. Also, that was the day they both had a bit of a lie-in and eventually I would always sneak in and disturb their rest. It would be lovely to snuggle up to them, and then after a brief rumpus gradually push my poor father nearer and nearer the edge, finally forcing him to get up saying, "I'll make us a cup of tea, Gladys, and yes, Tuppence, I'll bring water for you." "Tuppence" or "Tuppennie" was his pet name for his daughter.

The next happy thing to happen was going to church. Rushing off full of anticipation, I'd know that after a pleasant time with friends and kind teachers, when I returned home, Mother's efforts would fill the kitchen and the whole house with a delicious smell of cooking. Our one special meal each week was our Sunday roast dinner and it would be almost ready. In these early days there was usually a nice joint which had been purchased cheaply late on Saturday from the High Street shopping centre. Whatever the meat was, there was always a crispy Yorkshire pudding to accompany it, with many gloriously crunchy roast potatoes, fresh green vegetables and lashings of tasty gravy. How we all tucked in and enjoyed the feast, but for one small child such indulgence had its price. Somehow, by teatime tummy ache would spoil my special day. A nauseous sensation frequently lodged in my chest, pains racked my full stomach and there was a nasty taste in my mouth, and it happened almost without fail every Sunday afternoon.

Now I realise those awful feelings were heartburn, indigestion and sickness caused by excessive fat. My mother was a reasonable cook but often failed to heat her fat enough, so the potatoes were saturated right through with greasy dripping saved from the previous week's orgy, and she never dried them on kitchen paper — we never had that in our house. The Yorkshire pudding too was swimming with fat. My parents appeared to cope with these special dinners far more ably than their daughter — at least they were never noticeably unwell on Sundays as was their small-fry.

In spite of discomfort and these tummy upsets, I was seldom really that poorly, so afternoon Sunday School was not often missed. Time spent there was always the highlight of the day, and the week as well, competing with the usual pleasant family Sunday evening. After tea on Sundays, Father would never reopen the shop or answer any knocks on the closed door. Mother would then find time for knitting or sewing, showing me how to do the former. Sewing was more difficult as I was left-handed and this made learning difficult. Dad loved to read his Sunday paper, the only day he had one, and he would read to me, or help with belated homework once Junior School had started.

One last remembrance happened much later, not long before the Second World War began. I must have been nearly 13 when Mother mentioned it. At the time it didn't really make the impact it should have done, nor did it arouse in her daughter the sympathy and support she really needed. Father couldn't have comforted her as he was too worried, and Leonard was far too young. Perhaps we would have all been more sympathetic if life hadn't become so distressing for us all. By then we were so poor that there were very few highlights for any of us; the threats of war were looming large on top of all our other ills and there seemed no hope on our horizons, only despondency.

Fifty years later I realise that my mother's lot was harder than any of the rest of us had had to bear. She was the sole breadwinner, the hardest worker, doing many things she least wanted to do, deprived of her real and desired role of caring for her children and ground down, like the rest of us, by abject poverty. I do recall her showing me her empty ring finger, explaining that she'd had to pawn her proper gold wedding ring — they needed the money desperately just then. Sadly when did we not? "I will replace it with a curtain ring from Woolworths," ended our conversation.

I suppose I showed some pity for her loss, but looking back now I know she didn't get real deep commiseration from her daughter. Then I wasn't old or experienced enough to understand her sorrow — a wedding ring means so much to most women. When we talked of this subject again when I was married myself, I really began to appreciate something of her hurt, frustration and desperation when she had been forced to part with this symbol of love and trust. In like circumstances I would have been heart-broken.

Sixteen years of family life had brought my mother very little joy, only slavery. She had had no strong wage-earning partner, as many women expected and often had in those days. In their impoverished state, her two children had become added burdens, her lot had brought many very exhausting days, weeks, months and years of work, no leisure and not one precious token remained of their ill-fated union. They were an ill-suited couple, yet they must have had some feelings for each other when Dad had first put that ring on her finger. Sadly, grinding poverty and constant work must have killed what little affection there had been between them.

CHAPTER
SEVEN

Additions and Subtractions

Poverty is no disgrace to a man, but it is confoundedly inconvenient.

Reverend Sydney Smith

Naturally conditions in our home didn't suddenly go wrong nor did we immediately become poorer after Leonard's arrival, but I now realise that gradually there were more and more restrictions on all our lives from then onwards. The timing of his coming with the effects of the national Depression increasingly being felt, made my poor father quieter than ever and less patient with life generally. Mum was even busier. As our baby grew, she took in washing again so that she could be at home and earn money, but it didn't work out. More charring didn't either; it wasn't lucrative enough and there weren't so many of these jobs about as money grew scarcer.

With no spare room now, and even less spare time, lodgers too were no longer a source of income.

Eventually Dad did most of the cooking and cleaning and kept an eye on the baby, whilst Mum decided to become a home machinist for a local clothing factory. The continual noise of her treadle and then electric sewing machine became the dominating sound in our house, outdoing Leonard's unhappy crying times. It seemed most strange at first to hear a baby's cry in our usually quiet place but we soon got used to having him around.

Leonard had some very special clothes. When Mother had to leave her last cleaning post, her employer gave her a great many beautiful baby things including an almost new little bath, cot, sheets and blankets, as well as the smart second-hand pram. Leonard looked very swish in the romper suits and two smart coats he gradually grew to fit.

It was very interesting watching him being bathed and changed; fetching and carrying became my main job for quite a time. I even learned to feed him when both my parents were busy. Taking Leonard out in his pram was much more fulfilling than it had been wheeling my clattering pushchair after Christmas. He was an exceedingly sweet baby especially when he smiled at his big sister — it was very good being my brother's nursemaid.

As the end of the school year came round yet again and the baby was over three months old, instead of catching measles, whooping cough or chicken-pox as had been my custom since starting formal education, this time I became very thin and tall and, according to the doctor, outgrew my strength — the only time I ever did. Then Aunt Lily, Father's only sister, to whom we had paid a surprise visit the year before, redeemed her promise just at the right moment and sent a very opportune invitation for me to stay with them during the summer break. Much to my great joy, both parents decided it would do me a lot of good to get some fresh country air after being unwell and it was quickly arranged.

Dad was left minding the baby for a day whilst Mum delivered me to Leatherhead. Holding my small shabby case tightly crammed with spare frocks, undies, socks and my nightie, and feeling very grown-up indeed, I kissed the two men in my life, and left the shop for two whole weeks to enjoy my very first real holiday, and on my very own too. Mum had the whole day off from dressmaking but it wasn't until much later that I fully realised how much she must have needed not one day but many weeks off work. She had so much to do now.

Mum and I enjoyed ourselves, almost as much as we had done before Leonard had come, and this time we went through the glorious Surrey countryside on an electric train. Somehow it lacked the thrill of the steam engine that took us to Liverpool Street, but it was a very much longer, prettier journey and I loved it. The gardens we viewed as the carriages rushed past once we had left London proper were much bigger and longer, and all the houses were further away from the railway lines than those we saw when travelling to Liverpool Street Station. Soon there were fields and fields to look at and animals to see — I'd never counted so many in the space of half an hour.

As we alighted at Leatherhead Station we both noticed the difference from being in Walthamstow. There were actually flowers growing on the platform, and everything was neat and tidy. The air, as we walked to Auntie's house, was much fresher and certainly nicer to smell. Dad's sister was alone, May was at her office job and Uncle doing his gardening at a big house, but she welcomed us very warmly and the three of us had dinner together. Auntie was very kind to Mum and told her to sit in the garden as she and I did the washing-up together. We walked round the garden, so much bigger than ours, and saw all Uncle's tidy vegetables arranged so orderly, runner beans, onions, lettuces, beetroots and Brussels sprouts — so many of them I'd never seen actually growing before, and all in very straight lines. We went to the end of the garden to look over the fence at the field beyond. How wonderful to have a very big rich green field right at the bottom of your own garden! Auntie, Uncle and May were so fortunate. Mum had to return to the shop after that and back to all her work, and I was on my own for the very first time.

Uncle Fred didn't seem so pleased to have a stranger in his house, but my big cousin May was very kind, just like Auntie, or even more so. We went for a walk together after tea and she was very pleased to find out that I had remembered the Ladies' Slippers, buttercups, clover and vetch — wild flowers she'd taught me the year before. Then I was allowed to see her bedroom and some of her very special treasures. I loved the china sheep and little shepherdess on her dressing table. There were lots of photographs of our grandparents and aunties and uncles beside her bed. Then she showed me some of the clever sewing she did and beautiful embroidery put away for when she married and had a home of her own.

The thing I liked best was the very pretty nightie case sitting so attractively near the head of her bed. It was made of pure white satin (just my favourite material at that stage), stitched cleverly with white silk thread and trimmed with fine lace. Apart from the burning desire to have a special front room like other people, this was the first time I really coveted someone else's possessions, and I did want a nightie case just like May's — she was so clever to make it herself. The one certain thing was I'd never be able to make one myself.

Auntie had a front room too, but whilst I was there it was only used once, when May's young man Reg came to see them on Sunday. Otherwise we all sat in the room called the dining room. That was a very pleasant room because it had two glass doors, French doors, which opened into their lovely garden. As it was very hot during my stay, these doors were always opened and they made the house really cool. Fortunately, too, there was plenty of that delicious lemonade already sampled on my previous visit and much needed during that thirsty period. In spite of having a strong bladder and no problems, the urge to pop frequently to the novelty of a proper bathroom also returned. They were all so very lucky not to have to go into the garden, and round the corner in the dark, to go to the lavatory.

We never had supper at home, but cheese, beetroot, tomatoes and bread and butter, plus a cake, washed

109

down with lemonade put off bedtime a bit longer and made me feel even more grown up. Then May escorted me to the bathroom to wash; I think she feared I might take root there otherwise. The cosy box room was to be mine for the holiday. How I loved exploring Auntie's house. In this room there was a curtained corner cupboard for my dresses and a wicker chest for my other clothes. Also, several pictures of country gardens hung on the walls. How comfortably my bare feet sank into the deep, fluffy bedside rug. Yes, it was certainly a nice house. My big cousin hunted out two books in case I'd like to read them if I woke up early. She kissed me and switched on the electric light, telling me, "Auntie will be up in a few minutes to tuck you in." How rich they must be not to have candles when they went to bed.

Soon I was completely alone! It had proved to be a very busy and exciting day, until I began to start feeling strange. A lumpy sensation came up in my throat and tears filled my eyes. Auntie's house was very, very nice but it wasn't our shop and this wasn't my bedroom. That was a long way away and I really wanted my parents and my little brother. Oh how much I wanted them! Unconsciousness didn't come easily, although I was worn out with excitement, and now home-sickness overcame me and I cried myself to sleep.

Suddenly I woke, the pillow seemed slightly damp — had I wetted the bed? What would Auntie say! Then commonsense told me that it was moisture from my weeping, but it did frighten me. Silence enveloped the whole room. Tossing and turning followed and then, at

110

last, oblivion, and in the morning all was dry. Thankfully not a word had been spoken, and thankfully I had not called out! No-one had been disturbed. Perhaps it would be a good holiday after all. Optimism had overtaken home-sickness.

Jumping out of bed I started the bathroom pilgrimage. Later I dusted Auntie's dining room and swept the kitchen floor. We both went to Leatherhead shopping in the afternoon and she bought me two pairs of patterned ankle socks, just the type they wore at school. Uncle was in the garden after tea; gathering up the weeds he'd put on the path, I threw them on the prepared bonfire and stayed and watched him light the garden waste. That seemed to please him, and he liked me better after I'd helped him. The next day they both took me to Godalming to see Uncle Ern and Auntie Agnes whose bridesmaid I'd been over four years before. During the rest of my stay we had lots of interesting walks in Leatherhead and if they were both busy, a little park just round the corner with swings and roundabouts kept me active. I became quite expert at putting one arm through a looped rope fixed high up on a pole and running round, frantically swinging my legs up and out.

Reg, May's fiancé, proved to be a very jokey, funny type of grown-up, the sort of person children liked. He came to see May very often in the evenings and was most kind to her shy awkward cousin, who soon appreciated his humour. He was always saying my laces were undone and they weren't, or there was a spider on me, which I hated, but that wasn't true either. One sandal went missing, only to be found at the front door, just in time to go out. The purse I knew to be in my blazer pocket turned up in my bed with more pennies in it than there had been before getting mislaid. He was a kind, funny grown-up and I really liked him.

Now I realise how generous and thoughtful they both were to give up some of their precious time together to entertain so happily a little girl they really didn't know. By far the best day of my holiday, though, was the one we three spent at Chessington Zoo. It was paradise, except for the wasps which buzzed around our picnic tea. Until that visit I hadn't understood how large bears, lions and tigers were. Reg suggested we had an elephant ride together, and very bumpy that proved to be. The splendidly high slides with humps in them were free and almost worn flat by me, I am sure, so many turns were enjoyed. Yet the chimpanzees' tea party was the climax of the day. They were very funny, putting plates on their heads and throwing tea at each other. May took several photographs of us, which she promised to send to me when I returned home.

All too soon the last trip to the park was over, and Reg and I had played the final game of cricket. May sorted out several more books and made me a little sun-dress, and these were put in a bag — my case was already full to overflowing. Then Mum arrived to collect her daughter; it was lovely to see her. After dinner the goodbyes were said — I'd really thanked them properly several times — then May gave me an interesting parcel to open on the train.

How lovely it was to be with Mum again and there was much to tell her. Then the package was remembered. Opening it carefully, there in tissue paper was an exact replica of that coveted nightie case. With the snaps, and all my happy memories and then that surprise, all these things constantly told me that the fairy-tale break hadn't been a dream. It had all truly happened, and from then on I became addicted to country holidays with my kind relations.

However, it was good to return home and be in Walthamstow once more. Leatherhead was beautiful and Auntie's house was beautiful with a marvellous bathroom, but the shop was my home and it was nice to be back with my mother and my father and, of course, my baby brother who did need his big sister to take him out. Then I remembered as well that school would soon be starting again. What a lucky girl I was.

The winter following Leonard's arrival must have been a very chilly one. At least it was the first time I remember feeling really cold, and we all seemed to suffer the results of being so affected. There were several reasons that could have caused this. It might have been that Mother had had less time to knit us all warm woollies; most of our clothes were now old, second hand ones and my parents' attire was very well-worn. Perhaps the old stove was less efficient, or maybe it was just a very severe spell; probably it was a mixture of all these factors. Anyway, I recall particularly clearly that it was suddenly quite an arduous and anxious period for all of us from January onwards.

Heating and hot water were the first problems, as we had not used the kitchen range since the chimney caught alight. There was only the oil heater to sit round and warm up the room, and it only heated one small kettle of water after a long while. What's more, the wick began to need constant attention to keep it working efficiently. Dad wasn't very practical, as I've already mentioned, and it often smoked, leaving a nasty black patch on the ceiling, and sometimes gave out unpleasant fumes. Fuel for the old copper was not included in the tight budget now, so the scullery was always cold and there was no great quantity of hot water for the weekly bath night as had been the custom. Having a baby in the house required fairly frequent washes, if only in a little container, and he produced lots of washing which meant water being boiled on the old gas stove, and that had to be paid for too.

Money was getting tighter and Father stipulated that we three older ones could only put on one kettle between us night and morning for our ablutions, otherwise cold water had to suffice, even for the washing up after dinner, unless the saucepans were very greasy. To young folk today that must seem a most unpleasant situation, but there wasn't Social Security in those days and money was never very plentiful even in better periods. My parents had an additional problem. They owned their own business, such as it was, and were supposed to be more affluent, and for a time tried most unsuccessfully to keep up appearances.

Cold winds, cold water and inadequate drying made my face sore and red; my hands became very chapped, and it was much harder to present clean nails for the after-prayers inspection. Shoes were seldom cleaned — there was very little polish. Our weekly baths now happened once every two or three weeks, and we used the smaller stand-up bath so that less water was required from saucepans heated on the gas stove. Dad walked about the rooms more and did exercises sometimes. His headaches increased and he had pains in his face. How much my poor mother must have suffered, sitting at her machine hour after hour in a poorly heated room! She developed many irritating chilblains and had a lot of backache. At least I was young and could run about, and was at school in a warm classroom a lot of the time.

My father eventually had so many disturbed nights, which we found was caused by raging toothache, that he had to visit the dentist. He was loath to do this because of the expense resulting from excessive bleeding, and, as he expected, the extractions caused a great loss of blood. He had often had dreadful nosebleeds, which took ages to stem. I recall Mother putting cold scissors on his neck many times and he would pinch his nose desperately as a remedy for these situations. This new difficulty with his teeth was even harder to control, resulting in several visits to the dentist before the haemorrhaging ceased. Dramatically his daughter thought he was going to bleed to death and cried a lot; but after three days things began to improve. However, he was exceedingly weak and looked ghastly.

All three of us caught colds, but fortunately I never missed going to school. Then, probably as a result of her sedentary life and the cold conditions, Mother developed pleurisy and was out of action for some time. This was much more serious for the family as it meant there was no money coming into the coffers except what the shop produced, and the sales there were dropping all the time. In many ways this was the most devastating blow for my parents, and I'm sure they never really recovered from the strain on our resources when Mum was unable to work. It seemed to be just one thing after another, which is often the way life happens for poor people, and this last blow was the straw that broke the camel's back.

Father found it hard to cope with the shop (even with its spasmodic custom), plus two young children, the cleaning, washing, cooking, and a sick wife, and no spare cash to help with extra needs like medicines, doctor's bills and real warmth. He was very worried, for the bottom of our fairly safe, though impoverished, world was dropping away fast and real poverty was rearing its ugly head. Then to cap it all, when Mother had just about recovered and was struggling to get back into the routine of work once more, Leonard was taken very poorly.

Looking back to those agonising days it seems that Leonard had a bad attack of enteritis, probably brought on by failing hygiene standards. However, as on many other occasions, Mum never wanted to talk about these times when I was older, when I would have liked to get the facts really correct. No doubt they were all so disturbing and unpleasant that she wanted to forget them entirely and put them right out of her mind. I do remember being appalled by the number of dirty nappies my little brother soiled, and how frantic we all were after a whole day and night of his piteous crying. He wouldn't eat, didn't sleep, and not one of us could comfort him.

Although until that winter none of us had been to the doctor, except me when I had outgrown my strength and had had the usual childish complaints, we accumulated very big health bills in those last months. Sadly, since the baby's coming, Father had not continued Hospital Savings Association contributions, just when we needed that help most. Yet of course at this desperate stage the physician was called in again. Nothing as awful as these continual upsets and bouts of ill health had ever happened to us before and I remember feeling truly apprehensive.

Unhappily too, in that brooding atmosphere, thoughts concerning death again recurred. My dear little cat had died when he became ill, Mum and Dad had nearly done so quite recently according to my present state of mind, and now my little brother really might. This rather dismal and dramatic outlook may have been coloured by my recent reading material. One of my parents' old Sunday School prizes was called "Froggy's Little Brother". This was about an orphaned family living in a one-room slum without parents, very little furniture, no proper bed, and no food or heating in extremely wintry weather. Of course, eventually I went on to rationalise our position. We were a family blessed with two parents, had proper beds to sleep in and an oil stove to help keep us warm. Yet I still continued to worry. Mum had been quite ill and my little brother was so very thin, and now after two days of very distressing crying was lying quiet and unnaturally still. What would become of him? Would he die like Froggy's little brother?

Then the doctor came and prescribed some magic medicine. It must have been magic as it soon worked the healing miracle. Almost immediately Leonard improved and slept. The next day, after being so lifeless, he crawled to the end of his cot, pulled himself up and slowly held out a stick-like arm pleading "bicky bicky". We were all very relieved. I jumped up and down, kissed him eagerly and rushed downstairs with Dad to prepare him some Robertson's Gruel, which was always kept in reserve for upset stomachs and invalids, whilst Mum cuddled and hugged him. Thus began his steady recovery and I returned most cheerfully to nursemaid duties again.

Another difficulty that started during this winter, which was to prove a recurring and intensifying one for the rest of our home life in Eden Road, was our leaking roof. A damp patch had begun to appear in my bedroom right over my bed and, with the end of the rain, this had dried into a brown stain. Now with the return of wet wintry weather it had returned and remained constantly damp, with drips falling on my bed. I began to dislike going to bed and had bad dreams about it. Fortunately, when the better weather came, one of Dad's buddies did a cheap temporary repair, and for a while all was well. In fact, with the warmer days, everything began to look better and for a short period there was a slight general improvement in our family conditions.

St Stephen's continued to provide a real refuge. Although I was busy entertaining Leonard and doing more jobs to help my parents, there was still some spare time to join in activities there and go to Sunday School. The magic lantern and rarer silent film shows continued to brighten our dull routine existences and enlarged our narrow horizons. The Sunday School scripture exams helped with school scripture tests and increased confidence. As the many months, and even a couple of years flew by, I longed for the day when my brother would be able to come to church with me. How good it would be to introduce him to my friends there and take him to the beginners' class.

Unfortunately, Leonard was physically a very lively little boy whose beginnings had not been as calm and gentle as mine. He didn't take so kindly, as his sister had done, to sitting still and listening to the well-meaning teachers, or to colouring pictures and patiently making models, even with help. It was very very disappointing. His sister soon learned that little brothers weren't so easily manipulated as baby brothers, and he showed fierce resentment towards my reprimands. No doubt I was very bossy! He was rather quick-tempered and probably too young for that situation. Anyhow, my parents wisely suggested that he stayed at home until he was a bit older. As Leonard grew, he became even less responsive to my ideas for

119

games — mine were much too sedentary; on the other hand, he began to disturb my more quiet play and great delight in reading. St. Stephen's became more of a retreat. I still loved my brother dearly, but his growing up, I began to realise, had certain disadvantages as well as great delights.

The influence of day school was gradually becoming more dominant; there were so many lovely things to see and do. Country dancing appeared on the curriculum and that I loved very much. It took what seemed many weeks to save up for the required gym shoes with elasticated fronts, even with occasional help from Mum, but at last I could participate and it was all well worth waiting for. "Gathering Peasecods", doing the "Gay Gordons", and weaving a "grand chain" became firm favourites. On fine summer days we even danced in the playground to the sound of the piano played in the open doorway. How simple, yet enjoyable, were our pleasures then!

Friday afternoons became very special to my friend Winnie and me as we reached the top junior classes; they had a very happy relaxed atmosphere. If the whole class had worked well during the week, and we always did, the timetable for that afternoon was most rewarding. First we sang songs from the National Song Book. I suppose to us then they were our "pop tunes" before radio and television helped spread continuously new ditties, and they were much more tuneful too. *The Last Rose of Summer, Shenandoah, Annie Laurie, Clementine, Charlie is my Darling* and *Dashing Away with a Smoothing Iron* were amongst our favourites.

Winnie had a very pleasing voice and was brave enough and good enough to sing solo pieces, sometimes unaccompanied. She did these very well, especially *I'll Take the High Road* and *Billy Boy*. It made me very proud to be her friend.

Of course there was a pill to take with all this lovely jam. The Friday morning's weekly tests had to be checked and mistakes put right. Miss Russell, our stern headmistress, would often come in to find out how we were all progressing. Then as soon as this chore was completed, it was country dancing until playtime.

Finally, after hectic scrambling to wash our grubby hands in the one bowl in the cloakroom, we'd have our sewing lesson. This could have been a detested bad end to the week for many of us. I was no seamstress and had no aptitude for doing fine running stitches round hankies, pinnies and huckaback towels that got more creased and mucky by the minute. White material and supposedly white thread became so grey in my hands. No, it wasn't the sewing that had such universal appeal but the stories related that were so satisfying. If there was no special assistance needed, or the pupil teacher was free to help and the classroom was very quiet, then Miss Fellows and our next teacher would read classic tales to their very attentive pupils.

They must both have had that wonderful knack of bringing the stories to life. I never remember anyone misbehaving, and we would be transported into another world. During these precious moments we'd weep over *The Little Mermaid* and her painful steps on unnatural legs, or *Black Beauty* and the race to get the doctor.

121

We'd delight in *Little Women*, the intriguing *Secret Garden*, and agonised over the indignities done to little David Copperfield. All these tales, and more, were revelled in by us. However it was *Silas Marner* that really tore at my heartstrings, especially when the miser's stolen gold seemed to have been returned to his hearth-rug, only to be discovered as the golden curls of a lost sleeping child. How that truly thrilled me, and the fact that he brought her up as his little daughter and counted her worth more than all his lost treasure appealed immensely to my moral senses. Here was real drama indeed. Oh, how we all enjoyed these glamorous tales!

The highlight of Christmas in the Primary department was the school production of "The Mad Hatter's Tea Party", and guess who had the lead? Learning words wasn't too difficult. Dad helped me whenever he could, and expressing them properly and with feeling was just what I loved, but singing *Twinkle Twinkle Little Bat* nearly lost me my part. It was my first time of solo singing in public and I was very nervous. My long-suffering parents must have found the constant practising almost as ear-splitting and ear-cringing as having a learner violinist in the house, but, with Mum's help, this time somehow the role was maintained. Miss Fellows' adapted silk pyjamas and a top hat (plus the 10/6 price tag) borrowed from Miss Russell proved to be a very convincing outfit and the performance was quite successful. My real pleasure was, however, very diluted by the fact that Mother was too busy to attend, and knowing she really wanted to come and couldn't just added to the pathos.

Lloyds Park House was a beautiful old building surrounded by very attractive gardens (although I didn't realise how beautiful at the time), and was a well-known place in Walthamstow — it was frequented by children and adults alike. The older folk enjoyed the attractive shrubs and pretty flowerbeds, and indulged in games of bowls while energetic young people played tennis on its courts. But most children hated even entering the front door of the old house for it was the place where the school dentist plied his painful trade. Mother took me there many times with the promise of a cream bun if I was brave, which no doubt helped in turn to ensure another visit.

Beyond the residence and park was a very big playing field where inter-town junior sports were held annually. So we pupils had rather mixed views about this particular landmark. Being quite reasonable at running and skipping, I often represented Maynard Road School, but never actually returned with a certificate. On the last sports day before leaving for my new school, however, I developed into quite a high-jumper. I was given a silver tie-pin for being the only pupil to clear four feet. Therefore there were high hopes (forgive the pun) for me to defeat the opposition in the town event and return with the precious paper. "Pride comes before a fall." Feeling very proud I prepared for the event, but the occasion suddenly became too much for me and my nerve failed. Three feet eight inches was my downfall; I couldn't even clear that easy height and from then on I panicked. A very ashamed and subdued contestant returned to school next day knowing I'd let them down badly. However my little brother still thought I was someone special and he was beginning to enjoy my story-telling.

CHAPTER
EIGHT

The Scholarship

No man's knowledge here can go
Beyond his experience.

John Locke

The biggest and most important event in our Junior
School life was the scholarship examination which took
place during the year that the girls reached their
eleventh birthday. There were some very good grammar
schools in that area of London and the competition to
get a place in one of them was very great. In fact, it was
so intense that our school was constantly inundated in
the higher classes two years before the examination was
taken. Maynard Road School had a very good
reputation for a record number of passes each year, so
children attending local private schools often left them
at the age of nine, and for the next two years attended
our school. Parents of successful examinees had to be
means-tested, and fees were paid according to income,
which seemed very fair, especially as there were always
free places and uniform grants for the successful poorer
candidates.

Miss Russell was our very stern but excellent headmistress and a very good disciplinarian as well. Our school had a very orderly atmosphere, and all the staff had high standards of instruction and worked well together under her guidance. Every one of her pupils was in great awe of her, yet few of us ever thought she was unfair in her judgement and punishments. Moreover, she had a very persuasive way of making us all keen to succeed and do the best we could. Each year all the girls in Class A passed the exam and even many from Class B. The rest managed to get to the Central School which was not quite so academic as the Grammar establishments, yet more so than the senior council schools — very few Maynard Road children ended up in the latter places. The top girl in the town nearly always came from Miss Russell's seminar.

During the final year before the scholarship the intense pressure increased, and we had special coaching from Miss Russell many times a week. There were constant compositions set and marked in great detail by our headmistress. She supervised spelling and mental arithmetic tests, and sums and problems had to be answered in record time. Old general knowledge papers were rehashed and worked through by aspiring students. Homework was set for each evening with extra given for the weekends, and very few dared to appear next morning without producing their best attempts.

Through those hectic days it was seldom peaceful at home. The machine was always rattling, Leonard was often restless and wanting attention when I got in; he had so little parental attention although both parents were at home all day. However Dad did try to spare a few moments to help me (which I think he preferred to do), or, if he felt it best, would entertain Leonard, leaving me free to do my preparation. My bedroom was a haven, but it was also chilly in the winter, and the candlelight used in the upstairs rooms to save expense was rather straining for the eyes. Doing my homework was not easy. Once I had a very unpleasant but salutary lesson in that matter. It was just impossible on one occasion to finish the evening's assignment and I must admit succumbing to cheating. Using a fountain pen given by Auntie Ethel and Uncle Charlie for my last Christmas present, I hurriedly copied the remaining answers from a generous classmate in a corner of the playground before school began. There was no time to work them out for myself. It was the very first time of cribbing and my conscience did prick me a great deal, but fear of Miss Russell's wrath was much greater.

However, it must have been obvious that there was no skill or craft in this transgression and no expertise in covering up the misdemeanour. Matching ink smudges on both our exercise books spoke clearly of my awful duplicity. Miss Russell duly sent for me and, guessing the reason for my summons, my legs shook and my beating heart sank into my boots. As I stood shame-faced with lowered head and eyes, she sternly rebuked me, yet strangely wasn't as cross as I knew I deserved. Was there a look of sympathy in those sharp eyes? Thinking about it now, perhaps she had guessed there were problems at home; but from then on it was my own work or nothing. I'd learned my lesson.

Both Winnie and I strove hard to do well in the scholarship examination, and often talked about how we longed to get to the Walthamstow High School for Girls. We made plans to meet at a certain place each day so that we could then go on together when we had passed that dreaded hurdle. With the constant lack of time and facilities to do my preparation properly, nightmares about that all-important day kept recurring. What would happen if I didn't achieve my goal? It would be awful not to go to the same school as my friend, and utterly unbearable not to attend that marvellous school which Miss Russell had urged us to aim for. To have to attend a council school, St Joseph's, was absolutely unthinkable. Apart from the ignominy of not passing, my infant tormentors were already there, and what if they all ganged up against me in the same way again? Who said that one's childhood is the most carefree period in life?

Our shop had never been a really prosperous business, but before the Depression and growing unemployment we had rubbed along fairly well. Representatives from confectionery and grocery wholesalers had called on my father knowing he would always order some stock. Now fewer goods were carried and the variety lessened, shelves had an empty look about them and salesmen never called. Overhearing my parents' constant anxious discussions made me very aware of our poor economic situation but, of course, I had no experience to know that many other folk were in the same predicament, and anyway would that knowledge have really helped us?

My once pretty, attractive mother didn't sing very frequently now, and even her egotistical daughter realised she looked tired. Who wouldn't be exhausted sitting at that noisy machine, struggling to finish the number of garments required to get the hoped-for and very necessary meagre payment? My kindly, studious father seldom smiled, and was often impatient with me, which hadn't been his manner before this stressful time. My parents were trapped by their declining circumstances. In addition, their little energetic and ever-demanding son, and non-money-producing, fast-growing daughter were heavy burdens.

Our scanty meals were extremely plain, and little housework was done. Our house became messier, even rather dirty, and there were very few simple treats with Mother these days. Father even allowed Len and me to play out on the concrete approach to the shop, and if I was there to look after him it was only a small step on to the pavement, and eventually to playing in the road. How different things were now! There had been a time when neither of them would have allowed a child of theirs out in the street, "but needs must when the devil drives".

Joining with some of the boys and girls in Eden Road, we learned to play hopscotch, statues, Queenie, Higher and Higher, marbles in the gutter, and we spun our tops until darkness fell on warm sunny evenings. Regular early bedtimes had now become very haphazard arrangements.

During this period my father sold quite a few little wooden tops when the allotted period came round for that particular game. There was a set season for all such childlike pastimes and it was uncanny, and amazing, how the new current craze suddenly overtook the previous one. These tops had round substantial stems with a metal stud fastened at the bottom. The wider flatter upper part could be coloured with bright chalks, making attractive patterns which looked even better when the whip sent them spinning very fast. We vied with each other to see how far along the pavement we could send our top and keep it turning and twisting. Len and I shouted with the rest.

Occasionally worldwide, and national, news did filter through in spite of having no wireless or daily paper. Since Len's arrival, Dad only had a Sunday paper, primarily to check the football results. Well-known singers and artists of the wireless programmes were unknown to us, and so were famous people of the printed word in the popular press. Gradually, however, the doings of Hitler became known through talks at school and my father's shop discussions. He was very interested in politics and could chat for ages on these matters with his special friends. He told us about George V's death, and the almost simultaneous demise of Rudyard Kipling whom Dad regarded as a gifted poet and good story-teller. Now, too, we often discussed current affairs at school to increase our chances of doing well in the general knowledge paper in the approaching scholarship.

After the royal funeral there was great excitement surrounding the coronation of Edward VIII. Father bought in a few small novelties like tins of toffees and cheap mugs, all commemorating that forthcoming glorious event. Len and I were looking forward to the planned street party, which public-spirited inhabitants in the East End delighted to organise. Then suddenly every preparation had to be cancelled and there was great disappointment because the King had abdicated. He wanted to marry the twice-divorced American named Wallis Simpson. My father thoroughly disapproved of the new King's attitude to his ordained position, but I think my mother had a romantic and secret sympathy for him. Moreover, my poor father had a real grudge against his abdication. All the money spent on the coronation's memorabilia was now wasted as it wouldn't do for the fresh celebrations of King George VI.

However, the fact that Princess Elizabeth might one day be Queen, and she was then a girl exactly my age, was of real interest to me and triggered off my attraction to national and international affairs. My father explained it was history in the making and that we were all part of it. That had never occurred to me before. With the renewed promise of street parties, and a special holiday from school to celebrate the occasion, 1937 was going to be a most important year for all of us.

Moreover, there were more red-letter days to come. We had had an early invitation to my cousin May's marriage to her jolly fiancé, Reg, just after Easter and, of course, that dreadful examination was going to take place during those special twelve months. 1937 was certainly going to be a landmark in our lives, or so Winnie and I thought as we chatted together long, long ago. Soon after January was over, Auntie Lily and the bride-to-be paid their first visit to our shop since that other family wedding of Auntie Agnes and Uncle Ern. My secret hope, nursed since the last summer holiday at Leatherhead, that I might just be a bridesmaid, had really come to pass. May was making her own dress and mine, and had come to give me a fitting. What a pity Leonard was too young to be a page boy.

Princess Elizabeth would have a special dress for her father's coronation and I was going to have a really wonderful creation for my cousin's wedding. There couldn't possibly have been such a beautiful frock, not even the one the princess was having for her father's ceremony. Made of swishing rustling taffeta, my current favourite material, even surpassing shining satin, it was going to be really long, right down to my feet. The colour was a very pretty pink shade, with a wide pale-blue sash finished with a big bow at the back. Round the collar and sleeve cuffs were to be bands of little forget-me-nots, plus a matching flowered head-dress. The "pièce de résistance" and the very height of fashion were the dainty blue ankle-strap shoes, much longed for by me. Auntie and May took me out that very day to buy them, threatening me, pleasantly, not to outgrow my pumps by the time the great day arrived. All my dreams were coming true, and how my classmates would envy me when I wore my shoes to school. I didn't realise then that by that time they would be dyed to a mundane black.

Then that much-dreaded scholarship examination really came to pass. Our hard-working teacher and the ever-encouraging Miss Russell were full of good advice and sensible tips to get us all through the test with flying colours. Somehow I think I was beyond hope; on the one hand desperately wanting and needing to pass and yet thinking, despondently, that something so wonderful could never happen to me. Moreover, Winnie seemed much more composed about it all and always received good marks for her neat, well-done homework. I certainly knew my efforts were often much more erratic than hers, but I did my best most of the time. The trouble was that passing or failing such an important hurdle would control my future life. Miss Russell repeatedly told us this (even my father agreed with her), and the enormity and seriousness of it all worried me a great deal.

Unfortunately for all of us, and especially my poor mother, just a few days before this tremendous event, the machine needle broke in her thumb. There had been the usual rush to make the deadline with her sewing, and with too much haste the accident had suddenly happened. She almost fainted and looked deathly white, and was obviously in a lot of pain. Mrs Hackshaw, our neighbour, accompanied her to the outpatients' department at the hospital just up the road. Len and I waited for her return very anxiously, and did feel for her when she finally arrived with a big bandage and spectacular sling. It was very sore and so bulky, and certainly hindered her speed when she continued to work the very next morning, in spite of being told to rest for a while. She already knew many bills were due and would need settlement. Dad had been talking to her about just this subject before the incident had occurred. They couldn't help it; there was so little privacy, but speaking about such things in front of the children was most alarming for the one offspring who was beginning to understand.

With all this upset and the general state of affairs, there was very little food in the house, and very few packets of edible stuff in the shop when the scholarship day dawned. Two small helpings of gruel, the only remains in the last packet of such invalid food we were ever to have in our store cupboard, were made up with the sterilised milk for Len and myself. All our parents had that morning was a cup of tea until I returned for midday dinner, and then we all shared a tin of soup before I returned to school for the final section of the exam. I particularly remember our helping was very small and the bread was rather stale.

When I started out in the morning they all wished me good luck, even my brother. Winnie and I met and went on together, strangely subdued and quiet. We went through St Mary's churchyard, which then bordered a local dairy, still possessing a few fields in a built-up area where cattle grazed. The firm had a very memorable slogan advertising the milk they sold. On the delivery bottle was the outline of a stork carrying in its beak a new-born baby suspended in a shawl, and underneath the caption read, "Another customer for

Hitchmans". That always struck me as being quite funny and clever.

The actual churchyard was railed around, with only a narrow entrance for pedestrians — no traffic intruded upon the quiet graves and it was a peaceful place in those days. Also it was a short cut through to the road and then into the Grammar School. The church seemed very old to me and had a battlement-type tower. Later on I realised that it wasn't really that old, as religious buildings go, but it spoke history to me. However, that morning other thoughts filled both our minds as we hurried through to reach our destination.

The Walthamstow Girls' High School lay back from the road, and we two friends entered intrepidly into its portals where teachers and older pupils were eager to direct us safely to the examination room. There seemed to be so many girls like us trying for places in the Grammar Schools, and to my pessimistic mind all appeared to be extremely clever and intelligent. We were very impressed too by the big assembly hall where we sat the test. It was all very quiet and most serious as with pens poised we all awaited the signal to begin. During the short break we went into the playground and sought each other out once more. There was an enormous park-like area beyond, but we all had to stay on the netball courts and so could not explore the grassy parts and further attractions. Back we went to the continuing tests, having scarcely mentioned the papers already completed. Some examinees near me seemed to finish very quickly. In my case several questions remained unanswered but eventually all was over.

I've always detested post mortems; the next day was almost more trying than the actual exam. Miss Russell had us all in Maynard Road School hall and went through every paper with the proverbial fine-tooth comb. Several sums were wrong, but my greatest mistake, and the one really remembered, seemed to be on the general knowledge section. It asked for the name of the new King. I knew that it was George VI, and thought everyone must know that — it seemed much too easy to me. It must be a trick question, I reasoned, so I wrote, "His real name is Albert." Miss Russell was not amused. We were all very relieved when school life got back to normal once more, and that the frenetic homework had ended whilst we waited for the results.

Before that happened, there was May's wedding to enjoy. Leonard was considered too young to appreciate such an event so he and Dad were left together while Mum and I went very early, plus all my finery except the dress, which my cousin had taken back to her home to finish. We arrived just in time to have some refreshments and then got ready for the wonderful occasion. How we both enjoyed that day; the sun shone and in spite of being early in the year it was quite warm. Now I know what a lovely release and change it must have been for my mother from sitting at that dreadful machine. She was still fairly young and still enjoyed and needed some fun in her life. The ceremony was held in Oxshott church and I felt just like Princess Elizabeth would surely feel on coronation day as I sat in a very smart limousine with the other two adult attendants driving through the village, waving back to the people who had come to watch the very pretty wedding.

Besides feeling so swish in my finery, enjoying all the attention, gorgeous food, and great excitement of the day, May and Reg gave me a lovely silver bangle for my services, and this time I managed all my duties without recourse to Daddy. Also I wore a lovely watch belonging to May, which she had given to me because she now had a real gold one from Reg as a wedding gift. A lovely coral necklace which she also bequeathed me from her childhood days still resides in my jewellery box but, sadly, that cherished watch was dropped and broken by my little brother somewhat later. We returned back home, tired but happy, with that lovely outfit ready for the coronation party soon to come.

As usual it was not to be. Father hadn't yet told us, but fearing that he might be expected to contribute (free of course) food or novelties for the royal celebrations, which he just couldn't afford, he had withdrawn both our names from the Eden Road street festivities. Fortunately Uncle Charlie was the chief organiser of the party in Rolt Street and Mum, Len and I had a good time with Joan and some of her friends, but it wasn't quite the same as joining with folk in the place where we lived. Also, as we went very early all that way to Deptford, we were prevented from taking the bridesmaid creation with us.

Avidly I read everything that came our way about that state occasion. Fortunately, one of my father's buddies, a quite elderly widower who had a soft spot for me, was most kind and saved any used magazines and newspapers for me. When we'd all read them I cut out pictures of the royal processions, the balcony scene, state coach and important characters, especially the little princesses in their finery, and stuck them in my scrapbook — Dad's kind crony had also given me this just for my record of the coronation. Princess Elizabeth had become my great idol. She did so many exciting things too. How I wished I could swim (at that time I hadn't even been to a swimming bath), and ride horses as well as they said she did. I'd certainly never been on a horse.

One morning soon after that splendid day most of my classmates arrived at school waving important envelopes at each other and looking very proud and pleased. Winnie also had one and told me happily that she had won a scholarship to the Grammar School. Sadly, I had just known it would be like this. I was one of the few who had not received such wonderful news. What could I do? What would my parents think of me? I had let them down as I had recently let down my school in the high-jump contest.

Later, as I was chatting none too cheerily to someone in my class line about the results, Miss Russell suddenly jumped on me very vocally and said most acidly, "If you talked less, Elizabeth Cronk, you might have been sent a letter this morning too." I went home justly rebuked and heart-broken as well.

A few miserable days went by and then an unaccustomed official letter, not a bill, was left on the shop counter by the postman. When my father read its contents he was very quiet at first and took a while to digest the information, but I sensed it concerned me. Then the silence was broken! "You've got an interview, dear, another chance to pass the scholarship. Next week you go again to the High School for more tests." Mum and Dad certainly showed their pleasure, and how pleased I was to be able to tell Miss Russell of my second opportunity. This time it was an oral test. We contestants had to read a passage from a well-known children's classic and answer questions on it. What the book was, and the passages were, I cannot recall but, joy of joys, I passed! How relieved and thrilled I was, and my father was so very proud. The relations were duly informed, but made very little comment. None of my cousins had ever passed this type of examination so perhaps that was the reason little was said, but Dad was exceedingly pleased to let them know of my success.

The folk at Leatherhead and Godalming, though, wrote their congratulations and sent money for some of the things I might need in my new school, such as a pencil case, pens, a dictionary and geometry instruments. My godparents too were surprised and gave me a beautiful music case for carrying all the piles of homework they said would soon be mine. They hadn't known of my initiation in that field already under Miss Russell's tutelage. Uncle Charlie also warned my father that going to the Grammar School would surely turn me into a snob.

There was a medical exam soon after this, and poor Mum walked with me all the long way home afterwards, most embarrassed, as she tried to explain about periods and growing up. She found it so difficult and hadn't the right words to tell me simply and easily. We never really ever talked about serious matters together. How hard it must have been for her. We were also measured for our splendid green and gold trimmed uniforms, and I was over the moon.

Part of the long summer holiday was again spent at Godalming where Uncle Ern really took me out and about the area this time. I followed him most receptively. He showed me the very tiny cottage opposite the large vicarage and church where Grandpa had worked all his life as coachman to the minister, until a few years before his death, and where my grandparents had had their children. The minute artisan's dwelling (in estate agents' parlance) had two small rooms upstairs and two like ones downstairs, plus an outside lavatory and pocket-handkerchief of a garden, even though it was in a rural area. Our premises were small, but these were really tiny, Uncle informed me. The entrance was right off the street with no front garden, and it opened straight into the living room. How I would have loved to look inside and see where my father had actually lived with his sister and brothers when they were young like me.

In that little dwelling my grandparents had raised their nine surviving children out of a count of eleven. Auntie Lily had been the oldest and only daughter, and had been a second mother to many of them, especially to my father who had been one of the younger members. No wonder she only had one child of her own, my cousin May.

Uncle Ern also took me down through the water meadows which, with his parents, were talked about so frequently and wistfully by my father. The beautiful, peaceful memorial gardens to John Phillips, one of the radio operators on the *Titanic*, and a local man who, with many other brave crew members, had gone down with the supposedly unsinkable vessel, were also visited. Finally we walked up the hill beyond Cliff Road to the graveyard where my grandparents were buried.

Every night, crickets seemed to chirp continuously and merrily; how I loved it and associated it with my lovely summer holidays. The long walks by myself from Auntie's house into the town proper were also most interesting — much more so to a city-dweller than going through the crowded streets to the Baker's Arms or the High Street at home. Here in the Surrey countryside were banks of wild flowers and lots of pretty gardens to peer in, some very big and spacious. The houses were much more spaced out, but there were some quite small picturesque cottages — there were no rows and rows of very uniform buildings here. Auntie Agnes used to spoil me when I helped her carry back the weekend shopping, and sometimes she bought me delicious creamy ice-creams made in the local dairy and, even more of a treat, sometimes a second-hand book.

The happiest memory, though, was of washing up, particularly after midday dinner when we had quite a pile of dirty crocks. There was always plenty of water here, heated on a more modern gas stove. Auntie could boil as many kettles-full as were needed. Uncle never checked her, as Father did us. It was my belief, and still is, that that very necessary chore is nobody's favourite task, but like my mother had always loved to do, Auntie also enjoyed going through her considerable repertoire of old and slightly more modern songs. We spent the whole time cheerfully cleaning and drying the dishes, and singing our hearts out. How my mother would have loved to have behaved similarly if she hadn't had to work so hard and could have been a housewife only, like Aunt Agnes. The carolling lengthened the procedure considerably, but certainly enhanced the task.

Instead of my usual visit to Leatherhead, Uncle Ern and Auntie took me by train to May's new home in East Horsley when the fortnight's holiday with them was ended. How splendid was my cousin's grand new house, and how sparkingly clean and absolutely tidy. The detached place was much larger than both May's mother's and Uncle Ernie's houses, with not only a bigger bathroom but a separate lavatory, the very latest modern version then of today's equivalent bathroom-en-suite . . . and there was another lavatory just outside the back door. As for their front garden, it was wider and larger than that of both my aunts put together, and the back one seemed, to eyes unaccustomed to such riches, a veritable park.

The furniture was rather sparse as yet, especially in the bedrooms, but downstairs it was all shiny and everything toned in and matched beautifully. May's front room was mostly blue — she loved that colour —

and as well as a big kitchen she had a dining room. It certainly surpassed Aunt Lily's home, which until now had been my yardstick for such judgements. There was only one very slight criticism (unmentioned, of course) from her very young cousin; there didn't seem to be many books. Surely someone as rich as May and Reg appeared to be must have money for such necessary and lovely possessions. I returned very reluctantly to 80 Eden Road. Even Princess Elizabeth couldn't have a much nicer place to live in than my big cousin's beautiful house.

On arriving back in Walthamstow, an unexpected invitation had stirred up a quite strong argument between my parents. The relatives from Rainham, Essex, whom I had not yet met, had asked us to attend the wedding of Winifred. She was Aunt Alice's 19-year-old daughter, Mother explained to me. Aunt Alice had died some years before from cancer, and my mother very much wanted to see her niece married. Father was very "anti" and plainly stated he didn't want any of us to become mixed up with that side of the family, but after a lot of discussion she won the day and we both set off for two whole days together in Rainham, the Saturday and Sunday. Mum would have two whole days off work and we'd be away from the shop. Fancy, two weddings in one year!

Sadly, when I tried on May's pretty dress it was already too small. Mum said I was beginning to develop quite quickly, but it was exciting to have time for an entirely new visit, and Mum had altered a jumble sale dress quite expertly for me, so off we went. At the last moment it did seem unfair that Dad and Len never had special treats, but then my father couldn't leave the shop and Len was too young to enjoy such an adult occasion. Somehow Auntie Ethel and Uncle Charlie don't feature in my memory of this occasion.

We were both in quite a whirl when we arrived just in time to see the bride completing her bridal dressing. There seemed to be many people coming and going all the time, friends, younger brothers and sisters of Winifred, and her older married kinsmen with her nieces and nephews. Mum knew most of their names, even if at first she did not recognise them, but all I can now really recall is Dorri who was just a few months older than I was, and her slightly older brothers Ernest and Fred. Also I tried to understand what Father meant about them being dirtier and messier than we were. Sadly, our standards were already falling, and their home in Rainham seemed much smarter and cleaner than ours that day.

Later I saw quite another side to my mother, which did scare me. With all the other wedding guests, we ate quite a lot of fancy food, which was most enjoyable, but almost all the adults drank a lot of alcohol and went on drinking and drinking. Everyone seemed to get noisier and noisier. Then dancing began and my mother was getting rather unsteady. Everyone clapped her and kept shouting, "Go on, Gladys, play for us," and she sat at the piano and played and sang lustily. An elderly man whom I hadn't seen before, and certainly did not like, kept putting his arms round her and kissing her, and plied her with more wine. She laughed and chatted to him for quite a while but eventually looked so unwell and ceased to play the piano. Finally, she sat in an armchair almost in tears, and so was her daughter. I was very, very frightened and the wedding from then on held no joy at all.

It was nothing like May's lovely celebration. There folk had also laughed, joked, sung, drank and danced, but no-one had fallen about or got really drunk. Yet how understandable now is Mum's lapse in these circumstances, if somewhat unwise. Those two days must have been such a wonderful release from all the constant hard-pressured machining she did day after day. No wonder she over-indulged. Moreover, she really loved parties and seeing the family, and how she enjoyed being the centre of attention. She was the only one present, too, who could play instantly all the requested tunes without music.

The singing and dancing went on and on until well into the early morning, then all the adults, except Mum, slept in temporary beds on the floor. We children "made do" in armchairs. I had already made sure mine was next to Mum's, where she had fallen into a very deep sleep. Perhaps Father was right in a way after all. It was such a relief when, rather quiet and subdued, we travelled back home. We never went to see them ever again, and not a word was said between us or to Dad when he remarked that she seemed unwell.

Suddenly it was almost time to go back to school, only this time it was to the Walthamstow High School. My goal had been reached, if somewhat shakily. A good secondary education, which my father would have truly enjoyed but didn't have a chance to experience, was about to be given to his daughter. I perked up. It was good to be back, ready for a fresh beginning.

My parents had been notified a few weeks earlier that the uniform was ready for collection, but so far the allotted grant had not arrived. Until that came, they explained, they just couldn't collect my clothes. The rest of the vacation flew by and eventually the last post before the only remaining free day had come, and still no money had been received.

That was breaking-point! Most shamefully I admit to showing off quite badly, but in self-defence suggest to feeling very let down and absolutely deflated. The joy and pride of going to my new special school smartly turned out like all the other new girls had disappeared. It was going sadly wrong. "I'm not starting at the Grammar School in my old clothes! How can I? Now I will never be able to go to that place after all. Without that lovely uniform, everyone will know we are very poor and will laugh at me," I sobbed. Following these rather dramatic words came tears of frustration and disappointment. All the pleasure generated by gaining my longed-for scholarship dwindled away. How I must have shattered my harassed parents by this unexpected outburst. I was usually a quiet child.

However it must have pierced my father's proud and kindly heart and spurred him into action, which was unusual for him as he was such a dreamer. He then did the bravest and most courageous deed I'd ever known him to do. The rates were due, overdue in fact; he had already received the final demand and had planned to send me next day to pay the bill. As usual there was very little cash in the till and he had no other savings stashed away. Mother's wages had already been used but he had managed during the last few months to put by, bit by bit, the money for that particular account. Instead of asking me to settle the debt, he put on his jacket declaring that he would go to the Town Hall. We were all so amazed as he left Mum and me to look after the shop.

Dad went straight to the tax offices and pleaded my case, saying that he could pay the rates, but that his daughter was starting at the local Grammar School next day, and the promised grant for my uniform had not yet come through. Would they please extend the payment time to allow him to use the rates money to purchase my clothes? He pledged to settle the bill immediately when the allowance came through. How he must have hated every minute of that interview, his pride must have been sorely hurt and humbled, yet how much more he must have loved his daughter.

My father was always such a shy, retiring man and was so very downcast by his continual business failures, but he desperately wanted everything right for me. I didn't properly understand the depth of his sacrifice at the time and what it must really have cost him, but I did realise he had been very kind to make that great effort. Now I certainly know what it cost him and I love him more dearly and am eternally grateful.

They did allow him that extra time, and all was well. He returned triumphant, and Mum and I flew to get the uniform. Walthamstow High School, here we come!

CHAPTER
NINE

The Grammar School

'Tis Education forms the common mud.
Just as the twig is bent, the tree's inclined.
Alexander Pope

The certain pride and pleasure Winnie and I both relished that bright morning as we flaunted ourselves happily before our families, and launched out together for fresh scholastic fields, soon evaporated as we nervously approached that strange unknown place of further education. We gazed up and around the building; how enormous and intimidating it appeared! Would we ever really find our way about the vast grounds surrounding it? Entering the tall gates for the first time as proper pupils, a feeling of awe slowed us to a snail's pace and a sense of insignificance overwhelmed us. It was all so much more extensive than Maynard Road Junior School. The playground was thinly dotted with bigger students of long-standing chatting confidently together. We were very glad we at least had each other.

Almost immediately one of a number of prefects, duly labelled, kindly shepherded us into the spacious

148

assembly hall where we had taken the examination and which we later discovered comfortably held four hundred girls plus teachers. Large though that number seemed to us then, at least the whole school could meet together. We felt a unity. Today it is not possible with well over a thousand children attending each comprehensive establishment. Yet we two were extremely scared by the smaller aggregation; how much more so must modern eleven-year-olds feel on entering senior schools three times that size for the first time.

Being keen and punctual brought its own problems. We were almost the first to arrive and stood timidly, not knowing what to do in that extremely big chamber. Feeling just like small peas in a very big empty pod we were even too frightened to talk for a while. The wooden panelling displayed the names of successful past pupils who had won scholarships or places into universities, proudly inscribed in gold lettering. We nudged each other as we noted there were still spaces, and wondered if ours would ever be there as well. Gradually, conspicuously shiny-clean girls in similar pristine blazers and tunics joined us, and excited and apprehensive murmurs could be heard. Finally the rest of the school marshalled behind the newcomers and calm prevailed; morning worship was about to begin.

The noiselessly gathered staff looked down on to the sea of tranquillity from the raised dais. Their number was considerable too. Our old school sported only nine teachers, but there, standing on the platform were almost three times as many. The atmosphere was filled with quietness and everyone stood motionless until suddenly the piano broke the soundlessness and thankfully we joined in the first hymn. Those much older prefects who had escorted us in were now standing at each end of the lines of new entrants. They motioned to any fidgets by stern glances and mimed movements to stretch up and stand upright and silent. The singing, which I grew to love so much, is clearly remembered, even on that first morning, as lovely and joyful. Now we all had to kneel down for prayers. This proved to be very uncomfortable on the hard wooden floor. Fortunately those petitions were mercifully short but most fervent.

Our new headmistress then stepped forward in front of her colleagues. She was much taller than Miss Russell and spoke more quietly but deliberately and slowly. Her voice carried well. About her there was a real imposing presence. It was so noticeable that if her new scholars had not already known who was head, without fail every one of them would have picked her out from the others on the dais. Like her junior counterpart, she combed greying hair back into a sleek bun, still the favourite style of most elderly female educators in those days. Her back was ramrod straight. I felt that she could never bend, nor would she need to with so many submissive slaves to rush to her assistance. An impressive lorgnette hung from her neck on a thick golden chain, and she raised it majestically at that moment to survey her flock, resting it longer on the unfamiliar youngest members. Winnie and I clasped hands. Miss Norris was certainly a most distinguished and formidable person, a more than typically austere headmistress, and the small fry were duly affected. At least we two friends were, and we gripped each other tightly as our eyes fell beneath her severe gaze.

Established pupils were dismissed to their allotted form rooms and we novices were commanded to sit while she made a short speech of welcome to us. The aims of her school were stated and some of what seemed numerous rules were explained. Whilst in the lower and middle school, girls were not to walk through the front hall to get from one wing of the building to the other — only sixth-formers and staff were allowed that privilege. We had to take the route through the outside covered way, so it was duly noted that favour was long deferred for us. Everyone must walk quickly and quietly along the corridors with the emphasis on "walk"; right by the wall, too, so that staff would have unimpeded pathways to their next classes. Furthermore we were instructed that scholars stood up when teachers entered classrooms or the assembly hall. Full uniform must be worn every school day, and there would be frequent inspections by our own form mistress. Teachers of specialist subjects like PE would also check and inform her if we failed to have the correct gear. All the grounds were open to us except the gardener's shed, greenhouse and work area.

We were then told how to behave outside that hallowed place. When going to and from school, full uniform must be worn, including hats and three-quarter-length white socks neatly pulled up to their full length. Members of the Walthamstow Girls' High School walk two abreast only on the pavement and step onto the kerb if adults wanted to go by. On no account could anything be eaten in the street, and conduct there, and on public transport, must always be polite and courteous. Complaints made to her about any girl would be thoroughly investigated and miscreants would be severely punished. My word! How times have changed in the "free for all" now experienced on the paths of our towns today.

Then Miss Norris unbent a little (not her back though), and seemed to relax. She even smiled at us reassuringly. "I hope you'll be very happy in your new school and take advantage of your very good fortune." She hoped that we would work well, doing the allotted homework carefully every night. We were indeed very privileged young people to have got into such a splendid grammar school; many aspiring pupils had had to be turned away. Finally Miss Norris declared, "The school motto must be your guide — 'Neglect not the gift that is within thee'." With these splendid words ringing in our ears she swept graciously from the platform and we were left to cogitate what gifts we had, if any, and what fresh ones might be discovered within these hallowed walls.

It was all very dramatic and impressive, just the right note for me anyway. Strangely it didn't worry many of us but did inspire quite a number to do as well as we could, for a while anyway.

We newcomers were then sorted out into three forms of mixed ability; streaming came at the beginning of the second year. Winnie and I waited anxiously listening for our names to be called; it took so long, and our initials were at the beginning and end of the alphabet. Sadly we weren't in the same class and went our separate ways mouthing to each other that we'd meet up at playtime. Miss Pope was my form mistress and I remember clearly her kindness and reassurance to all the new charges in her care.

The form rooms were smaller and not nearly as lofty as those in Maynard Road but were much lighter and very airy. No more double desks here with shallow boxes below the lids. Each one of us had our own individual deep container with plenty of space in which to keep books and treasures. Moreover, there seemed to be little thieving in those days, nothing was locked, and discipline was very strict yet fair. Miss Pope sat at a large table with side drawers on a level with us, not at a high old-fashioned desk with matching tall chair plus a footstool with which our Maynard Road teachers had had to manage. Moreover there were only thirty pupils in each form, not over forty as in city junior schools.

Our weekly lesson timetable was already written out on the wall-mounted blackboard, and Miss Pope explained how we must mark out the allotted paper and fit in all the days, times and subjects. Our first piece of homework was to do this neatly that very night ready to fix to the lids of our desks next morning. Beside the timetable was a list of necessary equipment such as slipper bag, gym shoes, house shoes, black knickers, all to be named for our PE lessons and ready hanging on our cloakroom pegs next morning also.

Then the term textbooks were distributed with instructions to take them home and return them promptly the following day carefully covered with brown paper. That was the second piece of homework. How my fears mounted. I couldn't do that! I didn't know how to. Ever a defeatist was this new pupil. Moreover, here was another problem. Dad didn't stock brown paper. No doubt it would cost a lot of money and I knew I had already been an expense to my parents. Yet, like a great many of my worries, this was unfounded. Dad had only had a delivery of cigarettes that very day and with his customary thriftiness had smoothed the brown paper wrapping and put it away with several other pieces ready for such circumstances.

Bells were rung in the corridors to warn us of the end of each session and it was playtime before we knew it. Winnie and I searched for each other and planned to explore the large grounds. First though we wanted to track down the very popular tuck shop. Knowledgeable girls in our classroom had already sung its praises. Each break-time it was set up by the caretaker and his wife in the aforementioned covered way. How the girls swarmed round them. My poor father never had anything like that custom all day, let alone in just fifteen minutes. One or two new acquaintances bragged that they would buy something there every day. We were both very impressed, but many whose homes were already touched by the Depression knew that they wouldn't be so lucky. When I mentioned it to Mum she gave me tuppence for the next morning but warned it wouldn't happen too often. It was thankfully accepted. Winnie and I shared a Buzz Bar during our next elevenses, declaring it was our favourite snack, and one

I always bought there when very occasionally blessed with money.

The two smiling sixth-formers who had stood at the end of our lines in assembly, encouraging our good behaviour during prayers, came to our form room before lunch. They explained that they were to be our form sisters. Their job was to look after us generally and act as confidantes if we had any problems — they would also look after our class during wet playtimes. Each year there was either a dancing or drama inter-form competition and they would help us prepare for these contests and also coach us for inter-form netball games and sports activities. Furthermore they explained that first-years were allowed to have camps or dens among the shrubs and bushes edging the hockey pitch during the longer dinner break, as long as we were careful not to harm the plants. These hiding places were lovely instigators of imaginative play, a refuge for loners and beautifully cool retreats on hot summer days.

During the first short afternoon session Miss Pope escorted her pupils around the school. How quietly we followed her lead, keeping near the corridor walls with voices hardly above a whisper. Sadly this changed as the term progressed, but never got really out of hand. Our first call was to the beautifully appointed gymnasium. There was so much apparatus with wall bars to climb and on which to hang upside down. One very agile fellow-newcomer was quick to demonstrate. My knees fairly shook. Father had always discouraged even head-over-heels in case I hurt myself, so right from the start I could be disadvantaged. Yet I'd always had a good report on drill and sports in the Junior School, and had prided myself about my prowess in this field. That gym was a spacious well-equipped room. Its highly polished floor reflected our faces; we'd not get any splinters in our seats shuffling along this surface. Gradually in that atmosphere, desire and hope returned. I'd begin to tackle the problem as soon as I got home by doing head-over-heels in my parents' bedroom which was bigger than mine. Perhaps a few handstands up against the lavatory door might help as well . . . and they did too!

There were quite a few specialist rooms, which really left their impact depending on particular interests. After she'd been on a similar tour, Winnie confessed to liking the needlework and cookery room best. Everyone in our party seemed keen on the science laboratory. We felt excited and greatly daring about all the marvellous experiments we hoped to conduct on its benches. How very elementary it would appear now by today's school standards. With just a few sinks, a bevy of Bunsen burners and a collection of chemical jars clearly marked, we hoped to set the world on fire, but not literally of course.

The sixth-formers had a special den of their own. Here more adult desks were not uniformly arranged as were ours. In the centre of the room was a large table surrounded by chairs, suitable for discussions or lectures. There was even a rug on the floor and a few filled bookshelves round the room. "We hope that many of you will eventually arrive here," said Miss Pope. She then left us to browse in the adjoining library until the bell rang. "Leave things as you find them and be very quiet," she warned us.

The library was a real gem of a place and proved, many years later, to be quite my most favourite refuge and work area in the whole school. Like the hall, the walls here were covered with panelling, but this was far superior dark wood beautifully carved in a Jacobean style. Later we were told it had been acquired from an old dismantled country house and had been re-erected in our library just before it was opened a few years after the school was built. How rich and splendid it looked, especially with so very many books. What a lot of them there were. I'd never seen so many beautiful tomes in my whole life as I hadn't yet discovered the pleasures of the public library. There were shelves and shelves of these most precious articles. To add to the enchantment, some bookcases were arranged in such a way as to make interesting and quiet alcoves, inviting students to relax and read. It was the most desirable room I'd ever seen and I vowed then to spend a lot of time within its walls. Later that day we sadly learned that only fifth- and sixth-formers had free access to the library, but that only whetted my appetite further.

From the library there was a door leading on to the verandah, which was part of the covered way over the tuck shop. On a clear day St Paul's Cathedral could be seen from this vantage-point. It also gave a grand view of all the pleasant grounds we had. How fortunate the school was to have so much open space in such a crowded capital city. We girls were certainly very blessed. How many of us then realised just how blessed we really were?

The hockey pitch was not quite full size, but there were four netball courts and that proved to be the most popular winter game. These hard courts also doubled up as tennis courts during the summer months with several additional grass ones. Hidden in a wilder area among the longer vegetation was a little pond. This helped with biology specimens, and there were many lively hopping little frogs in springtime. However the most unusual outside attraction was a Greek theatre built by some of the unemployed after the First World War. It had been opened in 1925 and christened by a fine production of *Medea* with Dame Sibyl Thorndike playing the title role. Several photographs hung about the school depicting this event. Drama ranked very highly in this establishment, much to my delight. It wasn't long before we new pupils realised that the study of the classics featured a great deal, and this marvellous concrete addition made many old plays and ancient history come to life. What a marvellous new world was opening up for us all!

Having answered Dad's many anxious and very interested enquiries, and ended Leonard's curiosity about the contents of my now bulging music case, there was a great deal of scurrying about to complete the many tasks resulting from the first amazing day at my new school. To begin with, though, my special uniform, bought by the sacrifice of my father's precious pride, had to be taken off and safely stored. It was hung on the outside of my cupboard, the day's creases having been smoothed out. Then shoes needed cleaning and so did Leonard's. Next on the list was the meticulous covering of textbooks. Fortunately my father had some good ideas about this job, and under his guidance, and with a lot of his help, all were carefully finished and put back in my case. The only book title I remember was *Ivanhoe* by Walter Scott; this I believe was our general class reader.

How lucky I was that Mother was also willingly involved. She cheerfully interrupted her tight machining schedule, found a bright odd piece of material, and quickly ran up a slipper bag which all the named articles fitted snugly inside. They both supported me so well and how proud they were! Those low, black-heeled one-bar buttoned house shoes must seem so old fashioned to children brought up in this present age of disposable goods and constant rush and tear and the perpetual wearing of trainers. Unlike today, it was then considered most unhealthy for feet to be in plimsolls all day and heavy outdoor footwear could ruin the beautiful polished floors, hence the house shoes. We were certainly encouraged to think not only of our own well-being but of the well-being of others, and to help care for the privileges we enjoyed. So we had to protect our beautiful building. These thoughtful habits have continued to stay with many of us all our lives — and were these really bad or unduly fussy instructions anyway?

Finally, the very first piece of actual homework had to be neat and ready for the next morning. Never would such patience and pains be taken over any preparation again. Dad methodically instructed me on how to get the paper measured and divided evenly, and then amused Len whilst I retired to the peace of my bedroom using the dressing table as a desk. The lines had to be so straight and the allotted lessons and days written down without one mistake. Miss Pope had been so emphatic. My newly acquired "rough book" grew considerably thinner that night; I dread to think how many ruined attempts filled the dustbin.

Thus began my Grammar School education. Our mother must have been very stretched at this time coping with her demanding sewing deadlines, seeing her home deteriorate and her children have less and less of her attention. On her shoulders fell the burden of earning most of the meagre finances for the whole family and shop. This extremely hectic life was further extended when her husband became very ill with a sort of breakdown.

Soon after seeing me settle down happily in my new school, my father became extra despondent and lifeless. All this was no doubt brought on by years of worry and extra recent stress. Seeing his unhappy condition, my mother insisted on him doing that unheard-of thing — namely going to see the doctor. He had been out of the Hospital Savings Association since Leonard's birth, as already mentioned, and, fortunately, after my brother's illness no-one had been poorly enough to require medical attention. Now money was even more scarce, yet he must have reached the end of his tether because, in spite of everything, he agreed to go to the surgery. The doctor recommended him to have a real holiday

160

with good food and plenty of rest to rebuild his weakened physical and mental health. Father was appalled at his suggested medicine and said he just couldn't go, there was no time or money to spare, but Mother insisted he must follow the doctor's prescription.

Here the difference between both my parents was most clearly manifested. Dad was the great worrier, on the one hand, pondering long and hard over every difficulty large and small, and in this way nothing definite was ever accomplished. Mother, on the other hand, was very practical and just got on with the situation as it was. Sometimes her solutions were not always correct, but at least she did something. This time they worked out quite well.

My father was a member for years of a sort of poor man's club or guild called "The Foresters". Fortunately he had continued his nominal payment. Mother encouraged and then insisted he contact them. If my memory is correct, and I'm sure it must be or he couldn't have afforded it, they eventually agreed to pay for a two-week break in a nursing home in the coastal town of St Leonards, near Hastings. We all thought the name of the place a good omen and promised to help each other while he was away and hoped that he would return much better and refreshed. He agreed and off he went.

It was so very strange without Dad. He never ever left the shop, except on very rare occasions, and then only for a part of the day. Now he was gone for two whole weeks. I missed him very much, especially to help with my homework. As for my mother, she must have been very hard pressed looking after the house, doing the cooking, caring for Leonard, who was not yet at school, the shop and the chores Dad mostly did, and of course keeping to her sewing timetable. Trying to carry out my promise after school hours, I did at least achieve my long-felt wish to serve behind the counter. Yet when it did eventually happen, torn between my homework, telling bedtime stories to Leonard, putting him to bed, and reading my library book, I didn't really care for that task one bit. Luckily for me, but unfortunately for our family needs, I wasn't very busy then.

Mum never really complained and was quite cheerful during these two pressurised weeks, but even a very egotistical eleven-year-old soon realised how much she had been left to manage. This was the time I began to tackle the housework, and I finally took over taking and fetching her sewing jobs and collecting her wages every week. Leonard and I rose to the occasion and were co-operative with each other. Mum was very pleased and rewarded me with several tuppences for Buzz Bars from the school tuck shop, and Len had sweets from the shop. As Dad was hopefully enjoying his holiday, I trusted that he wouldn't mind my extra pocket money.

In spite of the pressure of work and concern for her husband, the first Sunday evening after Dad's absence Mum took time off from machining and we three went to the Hollow Ponds near us in Epping Forest. Bravely, I thought, too bravely in fact, she hired a rowing boat inviting Len and me to join her. He went without any second bidding, but mistrustful and cowardly, her daughter refused. Somehow I just didn't believe she could possibly manage a boat on the lake, let alone with two passengers. Little did I know my mother and how she would prove her daughter wrong. Also, how I envied the two of them very much, as they spent a happy half-hour of unexpected pleasure together as I watched from the stony bank.

The following Saturday morning I went to collect her week's earnings as usual, but there was to be yet another treat. She told me to open the wage packet and take out some money to pay for this rare delight. I was to buy fish and chips for our dinner as, according to our kind mother, we had been very good and most helpful during Dad's absence. With great eagerness to get the meal, I ripped open the envelope and unfortunately tore part of the ten-shilling note. Minus the delectable nourishment, I rushed home in floods of tears believing that the end of my small world had come at last — ten whole shillings of Mum's precious and hard-earned cash had been carelessly wasted by me. What a calming relief it was to see her smile instead of reproving me, and, moreover, to watch her repair the torn note and feel her reassuring pat on my head. The return trip was covered in record time and the special meal was procured after all, but deep recurring sobs racked my frame for a long time afterwards.

We longed so much for Dad's return in spite of the extra little treats we were now enjoying. We had missed him very much and he returned to us the happiest we'd ever known him as he recounted to his family the many joys of his most wonderful fortnight of rest and recuperation. His vivid descriptions made me see the beautiful mellow house and quiet peaceful grounds where he had thankfully sat and relaxed in the sunshine. The food had been excellent — it would be after our restricted menus — and he did look a little fatter; but most of all he had enjoyed meeting friendly people. He had savoured all the chat, talks and discussions with folk sharing his own thoughtful outlook. Also his like-minded daughter knew he'd have loved, best of all, the spare time to read some of the interesting books in his room. How much he must have enjoyed that glorious fortnight!

What must it have felt like returning to a nightmare after a happy interlude! What a let-down it must have been coming to us at 80 Eden Road and all its insurmountable problems which certainly had not gone away during his absence. Yet for a while he did seem much brighter, recharged, and gratefully Mum let go of many of her added chores — we were back to normal.

During the long summer holiday I began to stay with my cousin Joan in Deptford. She had just begun attending school full-time. How nice it was to tell her about my big and very special one and show off a little. In fact I was becoming a bit snobbish, as Uncle had prophesied, but to vindicate myself, it truly was a wonderful place and it was really as much pride in my school as well as pride in personal achievement that made for fulsome praises. My godparents encouraged me to stay with them and liked me to entertain Joan during these long holidays. I was sensible and old enough to look after her for a while and take her out, relieving some of the pressure on them, especially Auntie Ethel. Soon, from their conversation, I learned she was expecting another baby. This fact, as well as looking after two elderly folk — my grandmother and Uncle Tom — was making her rather weary.

It was very pleasant and quite a change at first. They gave me more freedom, more treats and nicer food, much more varied, and more plentiful than at home. We'd go to the local park taking sweets and a drink, which gradually grew into proper picnics, quite a nice change for both of us. Joan was now more receptive to the retelling of nursery tales than was my brother. *Snow White and the Seven Dwarfs* was all the rage at that time, with much talk about the recent coloured film made of the enchanting fairy tale. Uncle thought it a good idea to reward me and gave us money to go and see it.

Unfortunately it was decided we had to go on Sunday so that the older folk could have their afternoon nap in peace. Realising that Uncle Charlie would have no patience or sympathy with St Stephen's religious teachings, I accepted sadly that joys often had to be tarnished with certain misgivings and guilt. We both enjoyed it very much anyway, but were rather terrified by the wicked witch — my conscience pricked me, after all — also, of course, this was a Sunday.

Later on we ventured further afield and discovered Greenwich Park and that became our favourite haunt. It was a bus ride away, just far enough to become quite exciting and venturesome, and yet near enough not to concern the adults. I had heard about Greenwich Mean Time at school and was very interested to see the 24-hour Observatory clock. The swings in the park went very high and the views were wonderful. The slides were fast — only Chessington Zoo had better, lumpier and bumpier ones. We'd often eat our picnic at the top of the hill overlooking the River Thames and Greenwich Palace, and leisurely watching the water flowing down below — we thought we were miles away from London and Rolt Street.

Until this time I could be bought. It had been very good to stay with Auntie Ethel, and be given money (lots of it in my mind) by Uncle Charlie, and to be able to go out and about with Joan and have as many sweets and ice creams as we wanted. Everything was such a contrast with my home. It was all so exciting and pleasant after the drabness and constant weariness of the shop. Yet after a while there was a different feeling, a sensation that something was missing, and it all became rather boring. In Joan's home there was less time for reading or writing than in my own; in fact these adults rather frowned upon it. I felt we were just wanted out of the way and I knew I didn't really belong here as I did at home. Perhaps it was a bit of homesickness. I certainly missed my noisy but loving brother and the chance to browse or scribble.

Leonard was never included in any of the invitations I received to visit the aunties and uncles. Mum seldom had the time or money to see her sister now, so Len never went there. Nor did she visit Father's relations, so they didn't get to know him either. I was known and big enough to travel on my own to Deptford, besides being helpful with Joan. Auntie Lily and Uncle Ern paid for my fare, and Mum's, to put me on the train at Waterloo and they met me on arrival. Poor Leonard never got a look-in and just wasn't really ever mentioned by any of them.

Soon an invitation arrived from the Surrey folk, and I was pleased to be off again in spite of not enjoying the London visit so much and wanting to return home from Deptford. This one was different. Gradually it dawned on me that though there weren't so many sweets, ice-creams, and cinema treats with Dad's relatives, they talked to me and had time for me and liked me spending time with them. I had begun to love the countryside because of their interest in it and care of me. There was also time to read and write when staying with them, and they never laughed at my quieter pursuits. This year, 1937, I also remember, Uncle Ern gave me his old wind-up gramophone and a few records to take home, and that proved a new pleasure for us all, though I think Dad and I used it most.

Until this period of my life, hymns, choruses and traditional songs, plus Mum's competition ones and the Edwardian party pieces played on Grandma's piano, were the entire range of my musical vocabulary. Now was added to that list, *Eleven more months and ten more days I'll be out of the calaboose*, *On a bicycle made for two* and *There was I waiting at the church* — scarcely the type to encourage musical appreciation. But *In a Monastery Garden* and *Praeludium* may, I think, be reckoned a step up. I thought, secretly though, the hymns and traditional songs were far superior to any of them.

The end of the first year report from the Grammar School pleased my parents very much. There were no prizes but my form position was well above halfway and I was top in History, which with Scripture, English and Drama were my better and favourite subjects. There was a good look-out for the new scholastic year too: brighter students took Latin and the less able, cookery — not a very kind comment towards cooks I feel. Still, Father was elated that his daughter would be taking Latin, but that subject and my general advancement meant that now I was well and truly beyond his power to help with my homework, and, I began to understand, that made him rather sad — he felt unwanted.

CHAPTER
TEN

Threats and Rumours of War

Ye shall hear of wars and rumours of wars.

The Bible

According to the worldwide and national news, problems were certainly worsening. The Depression and resulting unemployment in our own country was increasing rapidly. In Spain there had been civil war between Communism and Fascism. Italy had a blustering Fascist dictator and, what seemed even more worrying, nasty noises and very disturbing activities were coming out of Germany. It wasn't long before my poor father retreated once more into himself. He was extremely concerned about these aspects and our worsening financial position, and was in a difficult mood.

Blackshirt members of our English Fascist party began occasionally to come into our shop and they were not turned away. Father would chat with them, listening intently to what they had to say. I was naturally very interested and would creep into the back corner of the counter and sit quietly, hoping to learn something myself. They were very clever men and sympathetically played on my father's great dislike and jealousy of the more successful local Jewish tradesmen. Craftily they increased his belief that the Jews were really responsible for the Depression and so his own business failures. Of course I didn't understand all this at the time but did sense their cleverness, and in fairness I do know that my dad didn't really have strong racial prejudices. But at that time he desperately needed a scapegoat for his own deficiencies. So the months and days wore on with no lifting of the gloom.

From early in 1938 and onwards the talk of the increasing power of Adolf Hitler seemed to dominate all conversation. Eventually there were actions which gave proof to all the words of pessimism. The placards and shouting newspaper boys outside stations and public houses were full of the recent political manoeuvres. When I found and brought home a discarded paper showing Mr Chamberlain holding that debatable bit of paper declaring "Peace in our time", we were all greatly relieved; Mum burst into tears and even Father smiled. We were all caught up in the momentary cheerfulness.

At school there had been a lot of discussion in our weekly current affairs lesson. We also read and discussed the report about it in Arthur Mee's *Children's Newspaper*. Many girls had this regularly delivered to home but I only saw it at school. Everyone in my form was very conscious of the threat of war and the problems it might bring if it did come. We took sides in our class and debated the subject, but we were all influenced, I'm sure, by the fears of our parents who sadly hadn't fully recovered from the after-effects of the First World War. So there seemed to be rejoicing everywhere that peace was promised and all would be well.

However, soon after that day, things went rapidly downhill nationally and in our personal lives. The Cronks hit a really low ebb. Quite a few women at Mum's factory were given their cards and some home workers were told there would be no more sewing for them. We were in constant fear that she too would lose her job. Added to this uneasy state of affairs, our customers were getting fewer and fewer. The few we retained couldn't always afford to pay for what they ordered and pleaded with Dad that they might have the rest "on tic", paying the bill off gradually. Father knew from bitter experience how these debts grew and grew instead of being paid off; moreover, we too were very poor and could not afford to support that type of purchaser. So it proved to be a very vicious circle. There were fewer customers, so less money, hence not so much stock, so less trade — and so it went on.

There were several occasions when I'd be sent to the cut-price shop at the Baker's Arms shopping centre to buy cheaper two-pound bags of sugar. On bringing them back home, Dad would reweigh them and sell them in one pound quantities and at a higher cost. This policy also applied to various other packages. At least

Dad made a little profit this way, and did away with bulk buying and a larger financial outlay.

Things got worse for my father health-wise too. He grew thinner, ate less and was more withdrawn; moreover he did have quite frightening uncontrolled outbursts of temper occasionally. For the first time I can ever remember he lost his temper with his questioning daughter. What I'd asked him I really can't recall, but I remember my response to his sharpness was to be rude and cheeky back. Then he swore at me, something he had never done before. In fact he very rarely swore and then only a "damn" or "blast". We were both appalled and I'm sure he must have been as unhappy as his daughter felt, but he crept back into his shell and, being the man he was, we never spoke of this incident again. For a long time it was hard to forgive him but, of course, I eventually did and I hope he was able to forgive me too.

The clothing situation didn't improve either. The yearly grant for my school uniform was not unnaturally (in that awful climate) swallowed up in household bills. We did still frequent jumble sales but they weren't so thick on the ground now. Anyway, Mother had little time to repair old clothes let alone to make newer ones. Leonard and I were growing fast and shoes, above all, proved to be a real problem — even my second-hand ones were worn out. Holed soles were then stuffed with cardboard or pads of newspaper, depending on the room in the shoes. There certainly were no longer house shoes in my school bag and I had to avoid the teachers' downward glances in case they noticed outdoor footwear inside the building. Why did we have to kneel down in assembly every morning? There was no praise or respectful petitions from Elizabeth Cronk these days. I was only conscious of the sniggers and whispers of the girls behind, especially on wet days when the substitute cardboard and paper soles often had holes in them.

Saturday evenings never meant bath-time now and special treats were rare. We just occasionally had a stand-up wash in a very small bath. As for washing hair, that too was an infrequent ablution, and when it happened soap-suds were used and not shampoo. My scalp became very dry and scurfy as rinsing water was also in short supply. The shame of being called out in front of the form to take home a note from the head nurse ate into my very soul, and I nearly refused to return to school the next day.

Poor Leonard was becoming a very uncontrolled little boy. He had just started school and obviously didn't like it as much as I did. One morning he showed off a great deal and refused to go, eventually throwing himself on to the ground in a rage. He banged his forehead dreadfully, nearly knocking himself out. When Mum picked him up he had an enormous bump and had to be rushed to the doctor. Our shattered parents could ill afford this bill. On the other hand, poor Leonard was in great need of the love, time and gentle discipline given to me when I was his age. Sadly, Father had just given up on him, on everything really, and Mother was far too busy and exhausted to tackle the problem sensibly. How degrading and spirit-sapping real poverty can be!

Some time in November 1938 two quite amazing things occurred. The first was like this. Mum, as usual, was at the machine. I was getting tea, thick doorsteps of bread and marge, with haphazard help from Len; Dad had just gone into the shop when a strange man entered our premises, which was very unusual. He and Dad talked a little and then greeted each other most warmly, shaking hands vigorously. Mum and I watched them, extremely intrigued. Then Dad lifted the counter, unlocked the gate and led the stranger in to be introduced. "This is my brother Walter. We have not met for many years but he has just found out where we live and has popped in to see us." We were all amazed. Mum recovered first and offered him a cup of tea, but we were all very pleased to see him. Visitors were so rare these days.

He sat down and was full of chat. The bread and marge (all we had to offer) he declined, but enjoyed the drink and told us a bit about himself. At that moment he had just got a job as a storeman in Harrods after being unemployed for ages. He lived in The Cut by Waterloo Station with Auntie Nellie. He was a lovely pleasant man, a bit like an older version of May's Reg. Looking at me he said he had a daughter Betty two years older than I was. Then he left, promising to call again soon which he did several times during December.

After his departure Dad was very chatty. He was more lively and talkative than he had been for months and months. He explained that Walter was a couple of years younger than he was and two years older than Uncle Cecil, the baby of the family. Walter was the black sheep son we were very secretly told. What he'd done, Mum and I never really found out, but much later I learned he had had a previous relationship which had produced a daughter called Winnie. Perhaps that was why he'd earned that reputation. Auntie Nellie was his common-law wife. She worked as a wardress in the local police station. Naturally I was particularly interested in Betty, their daughter, and hoped to learn more about my newly discovered cousin.

Just before Christmas, Uncle turned up again beaming very chirpily. Immediately he asked if he could take me back with him to spend Christmas with Betty, Aunt Nellie and himself. My parents were prompt with accepting on my behalf and they were very pleased for me — there were certainly no special plans to celebrate in our family that year. I was thrilled and quickly showed it, then immediately felt like a deserter. What pleasures would poor Len and my parents have? But excitement won the day, and with my few bits and pieces away we went.

What a lovely time we had! Uncle Walter proved to be a jovial man at home too. Betty was a friendly girl and we got on really well which certainly pleased her parents. Their flat was below ground. It was quite dark as their windows were small and high up in the room so as to reach the rationed light. It was in an even more crowded part of London than where we lived. They were very welcoming though, and it was much warmer there as they had a real fire and much more comfortable furniture. They were so nice to Betty and me. Uncle took us to see the West End Christmas lights and go shopping down The Cut, while Auntie did her night police duty. We all had presents on Christmas morning and even I had some to give. On the way there, Uncle had put two whole shillings in my hand and I'd managed secretly to get some gifts down at the market, which made me feel more comfortable when they gave me surprises.

Betty was fair and quite a bit taller than I was, which was fortunate as some of her outgrown but quite nice clothes were turned out for me to take home. These included a very warm, orangey coat and matching hat which seemed very similar in style to one Princess Elizabeth had worn recently in a photograph I had seen in a paper. What was more important and helpful, though, was an old but much sounder pair of shoes that were just the right colour and pattern for school. I returned home with high hopes of seeing more of these three new found relatives, and I'm sure it would have been the case, but although Uncle came to the shop several more times, the war started later that year and almost immediately all contact ceased for quite a while. He did call in during the conflict when we had left, and although the tenant in our shop passed on the information she hadn't made a note of his address, nor had she given ours — we never heard any more news of them again.

The second unusual occurrence demonstrated most difficult conditions. A working friend of Mother's,

176

uncontacted for a number of years, looked them up and was obviously in great distress. She had recently lost her cleaning job and had nowhere to live, but had suddenly the chance of an interview for a housekeeping position next day in our locality. Somehow she had tracked Mum down and asked, no — pleaded, that my parents give her a bed for the night and lend her a half crown for the short fare next day enabling her to have a few spare coins in her purse to tide her over, hopefully, if she got the post. I felt truly sorry for her. I sat quietly and waited for their response with bated breath. Dad certainly didn't immediately say, "No, we can't help you," nor did he rush in with offers; however when Mum kindly agreed to acquiesce to her friend's pleas he went along with them quite sympathetically.

Next morning Kate left gratefully and cheerfully after very makeshift sleeping arrangements and just a cup of tea and bread and marge for breakfast. She returned later in the day to say she'd got the position, could start at once, and would repay them after her first week's pay. Dad doubted the truth of this pledge, I know, but Mum stood by her friend's honesty, and sure enough a week later Kate returned, settled her debt, gave Len and me tuppence each, brought us all some delicious fancy cakes and stayed to tea. This visit was repeated every fortnight with some little family treat, which temporarily lifted us out of our doldrums until the outbreak of war.

It was because of her generosity that we grew to love pease pudding, saveloys and faggots, which in those days were sold in most East End butchers' shops until late in the evening. Then she went away with the family she worked for and the contact was broken. That small helpful gesture given out of my parents' poverty certainly brought happy anticipation to two children and a real regular treat to our family's frugal diet. Kate was a very loyal and grateful friend, and my mother's judgement was proved very sound on that occasion too.

All through the winter months of early 1939 that old enemy concerning the fabric of our premises, namely, the leaking roof, returned with great vengeance, and suddenly I had two very nasty reasons for really dreading the rain. How I grew to loathe threats of wet weather and hate and detest all daytime heavy downpours and stormy nights! My feet got very wet when I outgrew Betty's watertight shoes, and my bed was often damp at night.

My bedroom was quite small for a big double bed, and however it was positioned, a large part of my sleeping area was often damp beneath that ever-increasing large looping patch. The first small grey circle had, over the years since the temporary repair was done, enlarged, spread and recently had grown into an enormous bulging dark brownish mass, resembling a murky ominous cloud over me. Every time it rained (and it seemed to do so much too often), buckets and bowls were placed strategically on the torn counterpane to catch the continuous drips. Unfortunately, many fell between the containers, wetting and damaging my bed right through to the mattress. How I loathed the sound of splattering water and was truly terrified that the soggy mess would collapse on me whilst I was asleep.

Dampness began to appear in my parents' room and also in Len's tiny little room leading off mine. Sleep became disturbed by nightmares! My frightened dreams were not of fire now, but that other mighty element, water. There seemed nothing much to look forward to that winter. Our lives were very cheerless.

My mother was also very concerned about our lack of money and poor conditions, although she had far less time to worry than had my impoverished father. One Saturday, however, she decided to have a rest from machining and accompany me to collect her wages. Before we actually went to the factory I found myself in the local Catholic Church. Although a nominal member of the Anglican Church since her marriage, during the Great War she had worked in a Catholic hospital and had become a Roman Catholic herself. Those facts I learned later in my teens. At this particular moment I hadn't had this information and really wondered why we were here. Then, as I thought about it, other bits and pieces began slowly to fall into place. I recalled the sacred heart pictures, the rosary and the references to Our Lady discovered high up in my cupboard just before Leonard's birth.

The priest was in the church and Mum withdrew from me a little to talk for quite some time. How my ears pricked up when he suddenly declared, none too quietly, that she was not properly married. Later I understood what it meant. Since she had taken her marriage vows in the Church of England, in the eyes of his religion she wasn't truly wedded. After some more talk, where she seemed to promise to return to the fold,

179

she then lit several candles and knelt to pray, suggesting I could join her. My embarrassment was great (12, nearly 13, is a very self-conscious age), but apart from asking me not to mention it to Dad, she offered no explanation at that time, then we went on to the factory.

When Mum came to see me in bed a week or so later she told me she was very worried about the shop and our money difficulties and her long hours of work for so little return. What with these, and the talk of war, she had decided to light candles and pray in the manner of her old religion. There was no follow-up about her rejoining the Roman Catholic Church though, and I don't think she ever returned again to burn candles. However, it did make me feel more uncertain and worried to realise that even my more practical mother was very bothered and distressed about life generally and our lives in particular. What was going to happen to us all?

A sad letter came from my Uncle Ern with news about Uncle Cecil and my three Cronk cousins. His wife, my other Auntie Lily, hadn't settled too well since returning from India. Life here wasn't so easy, she became unbalanced and was found dead from exposure in the countryside near where they lived. Much later we heard that Elsie and Jean, now motherless, were living respectively with Auntie Lily and Auntie Agnes and were working in their areas. Their brother Peter had reluctantly been persuaded to join the regular army a few years before. We didn't meet up with him again until after the war.

Auntie Ethel had followed her sister's family pattern; her second child had been a boy called Whymond, but since the summer holiday spent with them the year before, we hadn't met except for one day's visit with Mum and we didn't ever see Whymond as a little baby as we had Joan. Mother and Father talked about them, though, especially Uncle Charlie. He was a Territorial, Dad explained, and as the threat of war grew stronger they feared that he would be immediately involved. It would be a very unhappy position for any family in that situation, especially when the children were so young. At least it was a relief to know that our father was over fifty and so wouldn't have to fight.

Helping with the housework was proving to be a much more difficult task than I had ever imagined. The living area behind our shop had been steadily getting dirtier and dirtier. The hopeful, happier folk my parents had been when I was very young were completely changed, both now browbeaten and pathetic, and confused by circumstances beyond their control. Especially this was true of my father, and although not really understanding it completely, I did feel that they needed me to help them even more now, so I tried very hard to carry out my pledge to do the housework. With few proper appliances, not even a sound stiff brush, no mops, complete lack of warm water, no cleaning fluids except soda, little furniture polish and as yet not much experience, it was a very hit-and-miss method.

Mother told me to scatter damp tea leaves on the threadbare bits of carpet, including that on the stairs, all pieces too difficult to lift, then brush them up into the shovel. The rest that was removable I banged on the wall and shook hard. There were lots of corners I couldn't reach. Some furniture was too heavy or too rickety to move, and there was no wall brush to work havoc on the cobwebs. Flicking a duster up to the ceiling from the bed and chairs was haphazard. The kitchen sink badly needed a thorough scour with Vim and disinfectant, but the sliminess wouldn't shift with mostly cold water and elbow grease. The outside lavatory must have been awfully unsanitary. It hadn't been cleaned or attended to for years and, to be honest, I didn't know what to do there and was somewhat scared. Children learn by example, and I had had very little in that field since becoming old enough to follow consciously.

From the hushed conversation of my parents, it was obvious that they had also become very concerned about the unpleasant signs of most unwelcome visitors seen on the walls and in the bedding. Bugs I knew only too well, from books I'd read, indicated lack of cleanliness and the presence of filth and dirt. There were inspectors coming round the East End at that time assessing the number of people who should be living together according to the actual floor space, but we had plenty of floor space for our family. Our problem was that we could not keep it hygienically clean. Getting rid of these pests was quite beyond my knowledge and I was too ashamed to ask anyone except my parents, but how could I ask them? I really didn't think they'd know; moreover they were too worried and too poor to be troubled by me on that score. Yet their

182

daughter was extremely troubled. Every possible Saturday morning before collecting Mum's wages, with sporadic assistance from Dad if he was feeling well enough, we'd try to bring some improvement to our living quarters.

Then there was the washing! There had been no heated copper for a long time now in which to wash and boil our bedding and clothes. Doing our personal bits wasn't easy in our shallow sink with only a kettle full of hot water, especially as there was no proper plug — only rags for a stopper. Fortunately, once a month, which sometimes stretched to six weeks, a load of our dirty linen and clothes was sent to the bag wash. Although nothing like as refined or freshly finished as properly laundered articles, the clothes were cleaned far better than ever I could do them. Mum and I managed the ironing if and when we could.

Since the second year at Grammar School, I started to go regularly to the local library. The teachers had encouraged us to do this, and my pleas to go there after school were answered in the affirmative by my father if there were no special jobs to do at home. It was not just to borrow books to read (which of course I loved to do) for I soon discovered that it was easier, warmer, lighter and quieter to do some of my homework there too. Leonard always wanted me to play out in the street with him in the light evenings as soon as I got home, or tell him stories on darker colder nights. As he didn't have the regular early bedtime I had had, it gave me little time for school preparation.

Having made a good start in my first year I wanted to maintain this high standard, but it was proving more and more difficult to do so. I knew I wasn't clever, just a good plodder if allowed and encouraged. There were three-weekly tests at school and any scholars who fell behind their usual position in form were called to Miss Norris's study for a serious chat and I didn't want to be in that situation. The library was much warmer than our living room, certainly cosier than my candlelit bedroom, so trips were made there whenever possible and I hoped progress was maintained.

Winnie and I continued to be friends but we never had tea together now and saw little of each other outside school. Not being in the same form didn't encourage a deepening of our friendship at this time either. Sometimes I did call for her and met her parents, Grandma and sister Doreen, but she never called at our shop. Her parents were Methodists so she attended a different Sunday School and church. Pat Fearne was my new class friend at the Grammar School. She had been one of the girls from a private school who had come to Maynard Road Junior School in order to pass the entrance exam. How such an uneven friendship had blossomed I don't really understand. We hadn't noticed each other then, but now being in the same form with our common love of history, during the second year we became almost inseparable.

I continued to attend St Stephen's Church during this period and the more senior section of the Sunday School. At the end of 1938 a special part of the building on the side near the screen was given over for the older children. It was a bit like a little side chapel in cathedrals. Some pews were removed and replaced by chairs, with padded kneeling benches in front of each row, and a higher rail for prayer- and hymn-books. At the front end on the wall we had a picture backcloth similar to the altar area in the church proper, a table in front covered with a lace cloth and a plain cross in the centre. Here we had weekly Bible Study with Miss Hayward.

As the oldest and most regular member of this group, they chose me as the leading girl; Kenneth Strangleman, who was just a few months younger and the most loyal boy, became the spokesman. Between us we ran this little band under the watchful guiding control of our study leader. We participated in church services and worked out short ones of our own for midweek evening meetings.

Ken and I had just begun to notice each other. We had grown up together through the Sunday School but with this newly-shared responsibility we had become friendly. During 1939 we had been together on the church outings and went out on our own for walks in Epping Forest and local parks. Once we even took our tea out and picnicked together when I had been especially helpful to my kindly overworked parents, but it had only been lemonade and a few fancy biscuits from the shop. Yet for me it was a special treat and helped to increase our friendship.

As that fateful year of 1939 progressed, warning notices began to go up on hoardings in market places, shop windows and civic buildings, in fact wherever there was an empty space. These bills and pamphlets told people how to guard their homes, fight fires, give help to the homeless and injured, and where to get more information in case war really materialised. At school we admitted to being quite scared by all these placards and began to realise that if there was conflict, all our lives would be greatly altered.

There were many discussions at school and in St Stephen's Hall on Sundays about the rightness of joining in or of getting involved in a European war, and whether countries should fight each other anyway. Most children, probably influenced by their parents, agreed that Hitler seemed to be a nasty dictator and we couldn't let him continue unimpeded. Perhaps it was because we were rather too young, but I heard little mention of pacifism. However much we tried, there was just no getting away from the subject of the threatened European conflagration. Even the songs reminded us, and in some ways encouraged us, to agree to the conflict. *We're Going to Hang Out Our Washing on the Siegfried Line* was the one I remember best. There were more and more rumours of awful actions against the Jews and minority peoples, and even more proven reports too of German atrocities. My father had long since given up siding with the Blackshirts and was appalled by all the dreadful doings he had read about.

Eventually, the man of little action felt compelled to go to a local meeting on how to prepare oneself and one's family for warfare. He said it wouldn't just be the armed forces injured in this trouble, so even he was stirred to do something and he decided to attend the special meeting. At the last moment he suggested I accompany him. It was a most disturbing evening and gave much food for thoughts, unhappy ones too.

First of all experts demonstrated how we could sandbag vulnerable areas around buildings, then how to black out our houses and seal the doors and windows against enemy gas attacks. They informed us we'd soon be receiving our own gas masks, and we were shown how to put them on. What upset me most was seeing the special gas mask boxes for babies. How frightened little Whymond would be if he was still small enough to need that contraption when war did come. There were all kinds of devices and methods of putting out small fire (incendiary) bombs. Using stirrup pumps was one, and lessons were given on how to render first aid, especially related to injuries in air raids. All these horrors and the ghastly pictures of places and towns already hit by warfare made my worries about our leaking roof and my wet bed and shoes seem very insignificant . . . until the rains came again.

We became accustomed to seeing barrage balloons in the sky. They reminded me a bit of the Zeppelins in the First World War. Mother had shown me some pictures of these many times from newspapers she had kept long after she was married. Anderson shelters were pictured on posters, and men came round and delivered them to householders, and soon we had one erected in the middle of our back garden. However, when the gas mask arrived, that really seemed to say that war was

187

inevitable, yet I remember that it was a lovely summer weatherwise — the long school holiday was perfect.

As soon as the air raid shelter was built, Len and I went to investigate. He was very excited and thought it was like a little playhouse. Straight away, although it was a deep drop inside, he leapt downwards and was running and shouting about in the new acquisition. Gingerly I followed him, and knowing better than he did what might really happen and force us to escape there, claustrophobia assailed me. I was soon outside! Neither of us ever did go in that particular shelter for protection as far as I know. During the following winter it filled with rainwater and proved to be just an unused eyesore, but there were several others we were only too pleased to use to get away from the real bombs that fell much later on.

Just before the six-week school break started, my usual invitation arrived to stay with May and Reg in their lovely house in East Horsley. It was only for one week because of the pre-war situation, but I longed to go and I had a wonderful time. If anything, Reg was funnier than ever, and we all laughed and joked as if there was no trouble in the whole world. During this time too I became quite knowledgeable about the mighty game of cricket, catching my cousin's great keenness for the game. Of course, in the county contests we always supported Surrey.

The wireless was on almost all the time I was with them, not to listen to the gloomy news, but to hear progress of the relentless struggle for the Ashes between Australia and England. May and I were detailed to listen closely during the day whilst Reg was supervising his three WH Smith bookstalls situated on the local railway stations nearby so that we could give him Hutton's latest score immediately he came through the door for his lunch and tea. It was so exciting, willing Don Bradman's famous batting record to be broken; and eventually in a thrilling game it happened. How great was our jubilation — all thoughts of Depressions, wars, gas masks and Anderson shelters momentarily forgotten. Then quickly it came to an end.

Reluctant farewells were sadly made, and Reg put me on the bus outside Waterloo Station right to the Baker's Arms. As usual I was rather loath to return to 80 Eden Road; it was so different from May's beautiful pristine house, but it was my home, and I had gained in confidence and cheerfulness from being with those kindly cousins. Little did we know that Reg and I would never meet again.

For the remainder of the vacation, our family frequently discussed what should be done regarding evacuation. The Government proposed a scheme to remove all schoolchildren (with parental assent of course) from the large, supposedly vulnerable cities and towns, to live with people in safer country areas. Both our schools, Len's and mine, were to be involved. Families could be together, and that was the core of our argument. Our parents had already, sadly and reluctantly, almost agreed that we should be evacuated, but whether alone or together had yet to be decided.

Rather half-heartedly, I must admit, I thought Leonard ought to be with me. I loved him dearly, but these last couple of years had proved him a rather difficult brother to control and care for. Would it work out well for him to come with me? Yet without each other, maybe we would be very homesick if the war went on for some time. Mum and Dad weren't at all sure. They realised Len's wilfulness more than I did. Also my father, particularly, was still very eager for me to have my chance to do well at school and felt it wouldn't help my studies to be responsible for Len in someone else's home. So the problem went backwards and forwards with no decision taken. It was a very serious matter. Even I realised at that time how hard it must be to part with one's children. Deciding with which school they should leave London, was adding insult to injury.

Now, having had two children of my own, I understand much more deeply what an awful choice that must have been for all parents. To let them go in the first place, and trust the care of one's own flesh and blood to strangers, must be like cutting off a limb. The next difficulty was whether brothers and sisters should go together or apart when their education was at different stages and one or several of them would have to start at another school as well as live in a strange house. Hearing about the ruthless and devastating bombing of undefended Warsaw probably made up our parents' mind. The new term started early for both of us, and finally, after attending meetings with staff from both establishments, our parents agreed that we should both leave London, but go with our separate schools.

190

On 30th August we were to attend our respective schools waiting to be sent to unknown safer places in the country. Parents were instructed to send their children with packed cases, plus gas masks, sandwiches and with everything clearly labelled, including the pupils, just in case we left Walthamstow that day. The actual plans and date of evacuation were very secret.

As Leonard and I said our goodbyes, we all felt very sad. Our parents certainly were, but there was also a sneaking feeling of adventure stirring inside me. It sounds very heartless and unfeeling in retrospect, but it is the truth that both emotions, those of sadness and excitement, were present. Although rather a timid person usually, I was beginning to enjoy having holidays away from my drab home, with kindly relations in pleasanter surroundings, and evacuation sounded even more exciting, and a little more hazardous, than going to them. Ignorance was certainly bliss in such circumstances. Little did I know how long the absence from home was to last, and that in reality for me it would be final and I would never properly live in the shop again.

At the Walthamstow Grammar School we were all assembled in the main hall. Some parents had brought their girls to school and had said goodbye at the gates. There weren't quite as many children as there were normally, but considering the heartache caused by having to make such a decision there was a good percentage prepared to be evacuated. Proper worship began the day, followed by a talk on how we should behave on the journey and on arrival if it should happen. Excitement and anticipation filled the atmosphere so, wisely, we were then sent out to play, followed by community singing back in the hall for a time — then it was out to play again. Our sandwiches were eaten at lunchtime, and as no orders had been received by then, before dismissal, our teachers reminded us to come next day similarly prepared, with the added suggestion that a book might help to pass the time especially if the weather was unkind. We girls declared cockily it was all a bit of a let-down.

Both Leonard and I were with our parents that evening but the situation hadn't altered; if anything, Father believed it had worsened. I knew that it must be so as he had bought an evening paper for the whole of the last week and had become gloomier and gloomier. Off we went again the next morning duly kitted out and having bade them both a slightly less poignant farewell than the day before.

Hang Out Your Washing on the Siegfried Line, She'll be Coming Round the Mountain When She Comes and *Down Mexico Way* were sung so many times interspersed with renderings of Arthur Askey's *Busy Bee* song, that they had begun to lose their appeal. In spite of our fears, the weather was wonderful, but we children returned home again for tea. It must have been a real strain for all the poor parents and the teachers at school, waiting for the signal to "go".

Once more on Friday, September 1st, we got ready yet again for our trip; bags, gas masks and sandwiches all packed and labelled for the third time. I'm sure now that Mum and Dad knew this was to be the day of action. We all clung together much more closely, and Len and I hugged each other too. We all looked rather sad and forlorn, I remember. However, once at school there was much to take our minds off our parting, for action had really begun this time. Pupils from each form lined up in pairs, prefects and fifth-form girls in charge of a small group of younger ones under the form mistress's ultimate control. Pat and I vowed to try and keep close to each other. Winnie was there as well — she was with her own form, but it was good to know that she would be with us wherever it turned out to be. Doreen, her sister, was staying at home for the moment.

Chattering rather nervously, we were all assembled outside the school and marched in a very orderly manner to a local station where I'd never been before. It seemed a very long walk. Some anxious parents who had been waiting outside the gates, just in case, joined our pilgrimage, but there weren't that many, we being older girls. Pursuing our route, we met younger children going our way and more adults escorting them to the train. The roads became full of school crocodiles and a constant murmur of chattering children and very anxious-looking parents.

I wondered how Leonard was doing and if he too would be on the train, but although I looked hard there was no sign of Maynard Road children or teachers on the platform. The waiting there went on a long time. More parents got word of the news and came to see us off, but with their shop and sewing schedule, I knew ours wouldn't be looking for Len or me, and, in a way,

I was truly glad for in that atmosphere I might have cried.

Eventually we all tumbled on to what became a very crowded train. Our luggage was stacked in the racks, seats were fully occupied, and soon the engine began to chuff. We were off to a destination not known by any child on the train. In a way, war, not yet declared, had already begun for us.

Also available in ISIS Large Print:

Sing a Song of Sixpence

Hazel Wheeler

A collection of tales of life in Yorkshire during the 1920s and 1930s, which include accounts of the pandemonium caused by a fire alarm in a crowded cinema, a poor family moving house, celebrations for the coronations of George VI and Elizabeth II, ice-cream made of potatoes during the war, scarlet fever and bonfire nights.

ISBN 0-7531-9328-0 (hb)
ISBN 0-7531-9329-9 (pb)

Paddington Boy

Arthur Barrett

The youngest of four children, Arthur Barrett was born in 1923 in Paddington, West London. In this book, he shares affectionate stories of family life and school days, from accompanying his father on train journeys to Penzance to school lessons and playground games.

He also shares his experiences of London at the start of the war, serving in the Home Guard and fire watching. Arthur started work for the Paddington Telephone exchange in 1940, which was the beginning of 45 years of public service. He followed in his brother's footsteps, serving as a Radio Mechanic in the Navy until the end of the war, when he returned to his job as a Post Office engineer.

ISBN 0-7531-9308-6 (hb)
ISBN 0-7531-9309-4 (pb)

Down the Cobbled Stones

John Lea

A Cheshire farmer born and bred, John Lea was the youngest of a family of four, born on a small tenanted farm in mid-Cheshire in 1935.

His childhood memories are of the tough times in the 1920s and 1930s as his father fought keep the farm alive. There are tales of horses, water mills and the "Smithy", the exciting and profitable war years and above all his love of his life and the countryside in which he made his home.

John was struck down by polio at the age of twenty, and left severely disabled as a result. After a slow recovery, he eventually married and set about building the life that he had always dreamt of.

ISBN 0-7531-9300-0 (hb)
ISBN 0-7531-9301-9 (pb)

The Village

Alice Taylor

By the author of *To School Through the Fields*

"*Taylor has a knack for finding the universal truth in daily details.*" **Los Angeles Times**

"*There is charm and humour in The Village as well as a quality perhaps best described as loving kindness.*" **Irish Independent**

"*She has a wicked wit and a pen which works on the reader slowly but insidiously.*" **Observer**

As Alice Taylor put it: "This is the story of life in a village; it is the story, too, of a small shop and a post office . . . this is also the story of an ordinary young wife and mother who was sometimes bored by the monotonous everyday routine of housework and children, and who in an effort to make life more interesting became part of the changing village scene."

ISBN 0-7531-9964-5 (hb)
ISBN 0-7531-9967-X (pb)